Ancient
Technology

Technological Advances Made in Greece During Antiquity

(Uncovering the Advanced Technologies and Cultural Significance of an Ancient Civilization)

Donald Garling

Published By **Bella Frost**

Donald Garling

Ancient Technology: Technological Advances Made in Greece During Antiquity (Uncovering the Advanced Technologies and Cultural Significance of an Ancient Civilization)

ISBN   978-1-998038-92-3

Legal & Disclaimer

The information contained in this book is not designed to replace or take the place of any form of medicine or professional medical advice. The information in this book has been provided for educational & entertainment purposes only.

The information contained in this book has been compiled from sources deemed reliable, and it is accurate to the best of the Author's knowledge; however, the Author cannot guarantee its accuracy and validity and cannot be held liable for any errors or omissions. Changes are periodically made to this book. You must consult your doctor or get professional medical advice before using any of the suggested remedies, techniques, or information in this book.

Table Of Contents

Chapter 1: The Development of Greek Civilization

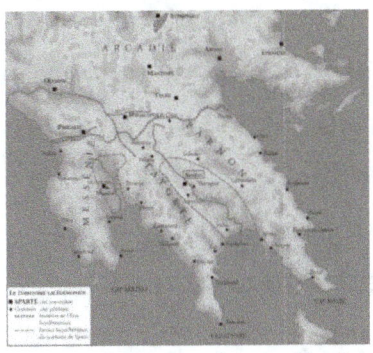

According to the archaeological proof exposed on the net website on line of ancient Sparta (and its immediately surroundings inside the valley of the Eurotas), the vicinity changed into inhabited at the least from the Neolithic Period. The valley of the Eurotas constituted a herbal strongpoint, because it end up (and to a point though is) a big, fertile easy, watered through the Eurotas river and ringed with immoderate, in reality impassable peaks that might most effective be penetrated with the useful resource of a handful of immoderate, without hassle defensible passes, some thing which contributed substantially to Sparta's next ascendancy. However, the unique settlers appear to were supplanted thru manner of what Herodotus refers to as the Dorian Invasion, even as a honest-haired tribe from Macedonia supposedly descended into southern Greece and the Peloponnese, displacing the close by population about half a century after the Trojan War. According to numerous first rate university college students, but, Herodotus's proof is to be discounted as he wrote based on myth and hearsay, loads of years after the events he accepts as creditable fact.

Another precept is that the Dorian people had been already present in massive numbers within the Peloponnese but formed the backbone of a downtrodden servile elegance, and the Dorian Invasion grow to be in reality an insurrection which delivered approximately the overthrow of the mounted rulers. Whichever concept is correct, however, what's first rate is that, of their own minds, the Spartans were fiercely Dorian, spoke a Doric dialect, and considered themselves pretty extraordinary from their Attic opposition from Athens.

As Homer suggests, it's miles in all likelihood that in the length of Mycenean predominance, which ended spherical about 1200 BCE, Sparta turn out to be subservient to Mycenae — as evidenced thru the fact that Menelaus, king of Sparta, is wanted to pay tribute to his older brother, and ideal ruler, Agamemnon. However, following the disintegrate of Mycenae, archaeological evidence indicates a marked boom inside the period of the 4 settlements which would probably in the end be assimilated into classical Sparta, a effect each of obvious balance inside the place and the truth that the valley of the Eurotas changed into by using manner of some distance the most fertile place in the Peloponnese, consequently selling agrarian expansion and a population boom.

Between more or less one thousand and 800 BCE. Sparta appears to have loved a period of prosperity and increase, notwithstanding the truth that historic sources from this period are non-existent and what became written down about it sooner or later is, to place it charitably, sparse. What does appear wonderful is that maximum of the eighth and seventh centuries BCE, Sparta suffered from a period of severe factionalism which brought on a country of quasi-lawlessness and disunity. It is probable that this changed right into a reason of the assimilation of 4 villages – Pitana, Limnai, Mesoa and Konoura – into the polity of Sparta, a manner which glaringly introduced on tremendous problems with the stableness of the Eurotas valley vicinity as every village had its own "kings" and entrenched ruling instructions, all vying for supremacy inside the new social order. It is a well-known idea that Sparta's famous "double kings" machine, in which two monarchs (just like the subsequent Roman consuls) shared same portions of electricity in order that, if one were killed in struggle, the Spartan state could no longer find out itself leaderless, originated in some unspecified time in the future of this period: the villages of Pitana and Mesoa had normal a faction which vied for manage of Sparta with Limnai and Konoura, and it seems possibly that the leaders of these two twin factions in the long run have end up Sparta's dual monarchs. However, this era of instability is splendid mainly due to the fact, in line with legend, it changed into at some point of this time (in line with Herodotus and Thucydides, all through the reign of King Charillos) that Lycurgus the Law-Giver rose

to power.

Bust of Lycurgus

It is difficult to separate the myth of Lycurgus from the real man, and absolutely many students doubt he ever even existed. However, to the Spartans, he have end up a completely actual parent in reality. Far from being a mythological being that end up maximum possibly a figurehead for a group of reformers and monarchs, he changed into the inspiration of all that it supposed to be a Spartan. His well-known reforms set up the bedrock of classical Sparta, enjoining (amongst various matters) all Spartan men who possessed a farm whose wealth become sufficient to hold their preservation to devote themselves absolutely to the workout of struggle and the inextricably associated subject of athletics. Though the Olympics of historic Greece were a harmonious event inside the path of which time no warfare is probably waged, all sports remained fiercely bellicose; the armoured sprint, the foot race, wrestling, javelin-throwing, discus throwing, boxing and the pentathlon had been all supposed to put together a person for battle.

Lycurgus also supposedly promoted clean, smooth dwelling and the abandonment of all luxuries every non-public and of the kingdom, permitting the Spartans the only "foible" of growing their hair lengthy. The argument in choose of those prohibitions modified into that no different adornment made a good-looking guy greater good-looking or an unpleasant one more terrifying.

Lycurgan reforms moreover granted Spartan girls an excellent quantity of freedom, and even though they'd no formal political strength, they had been advocated to talk their minds brazenly in public meeting.

Uniquely among other Greek states, the Spartans moreover lacked a foreign cash. Sparta grow to be in reality economically self-sufficient in phrases of produce and craft knowledge, and the Laws of Lycurgus said that forex debased guys, who might probable then in turn best are searching for for its amassment; better, then, to do away with it altogether. More controversially, the reforms additionally recommended the substantial publicity of recent baby children; male youngsters of Spartan residents particularly. If a toddler gave the look to be too sickly, weak or malformed to go through the trial of the agoge (the Spartan navy academy and allegedly some different of Lycurgus's enhancements), then the infant turn out to be as regularly as not abandoned to die.

The Laws of Lycurgus, regardless of whether or not or now not they have been the manufactured from a single guy's creativeness or the end result of a drawn-out political machine, gave Sparta plenty-needed balance. In the wake of the quelling of its internecine wars, Sparta started out to devote itself to the subjugation of its neighbouring territories, and the boom of its have an effect on sooner or later of the entire Peloponnese.

During the aftermath of the Lycurgan reforms, Sparta waged numerous a achievement wars in competition to the neighboring (however ethnically first rate) Arcadians, and their fellow Doric Argives. The wars have been a brutal affair in which masses or probably heaps of the defeated are stated to had been placed to the sword, displaced or enslaved, however the Spartans emerged effective. By round 750 BCE, they had brought Amyclae, Pharis and Geronthrae to their domains, making sure manipulate of the entire better Eurotas valley, in a warfare that emerge as less about one polis (metropolis-country) closer to the aside from it became approximately one ethnic group attempting to wipe the opportunity out. In this situation, the Doric tribes wishing to exterminate the neighbouring Achaeans, who have been the ascendant group, with the resource of and huge, because of the reality in advance than the

Trojan War. The success of Spartan palms on this struggle, and the ruthlessness with which they pursued it, first hooked up the basis for the Spartan tradition of victory, which could probable in subsequent centuries end up so cemented as to be definitely ingrained in every their very own psyche and that of all of Greece.

This military predominance modified into in addition cemented whilst, sooner or later between 750 and 650 BCE, two successive wars had been waged by using using the Spartans closer to their immediately neighbours, the polity of Messenia. Though the wars were ferocious (the primary war, in line with Tyrtaeus, lasted nearly a long term) and sour, the Spartans in the end emerged due to the fact the victors, and this ascendancy in their on the spot neighbours caused the start of the social beauty known as helots. The helots, who've been all of Messenian descent, had been indentured serfs (through all bills, without a doubt slaves) who've been positive to the land they have been born on. The helots worked the fields and performed all manner of agrarian and unique types of labour, together with the ones of armorer or groom, requiring a immoderate stage of functionality. Most importantly, this gadget left the Spartans simply unfastened to test the Lycurgan reforms and dedicate themselves sincerely, in their each waking 2nd, to schooling and making geared up for conflict. According to the ancient Roman historian Plutarch, whilst the Spartan king Anaxandridas emerge as requested how the Spartans dared to leave their fields within the control of the helots, he defined, "It changed into now not through manner of searching after the fields, however of ourselves, that we obtained the ones fields."

Nevertheless, helots weren't exactly normal slaves. Though their repute turn out to be lowly, helots were valued via the usage of maximum of the cannier Spartans, who observed the need to domesticate their allegiance, and helots normally assisted the Spartan military in war. Each armored heavy infantryman, or hoplite, have become located with the useful resource of a helot "squire" who additionally fought as a mild infantryman (usually as an archer or javelineer) and helped convey his hold close's load, repair his panoplia (struggle-package) and have a propensity his wounds.

The Spartans came to be completely depending at the helots inside the years to come, a dependence which, because of the truth the Spartans had been nicely conscious, turned into risky. In later years, the Spartans have come to be so scared of a helot riot, some detail which befell regularly sufficient, that they've been pressured to prepare a complete call-up of their navy outstanding with excessive rarity, lest the helots upward thrust up in their absence.

"At Athens, practical men recommend, and fools dispose." - Alcuin

Like most towns of Ancient Greece, Athens traced its foundation once more to the Age of Heroes, the legendary time even as gods had been said to have walked the earth, mingling often with mortal men. Athens's basis fantasy is especially chronic, cropping up within the works of a wealth of ancient historians in conjunction with Herodotus and Plutarch. It claims that the metropolis's population, even as Athens had first all started out to turn out to be a giant (but no matter the fact that apparently nameless) polis, have been visited thru Athena, Zeus's daughter and goddess of war and cognizance, and Zeus's brother Poseidon, god of the sea and earthquakes. Both gods requested the town fathers for the honor of getting the metropolis named after them, and that lets in you to make their offer extra appealing, or so the legend goes, they each gave Athens a present. Poseidon plunged his trident into the ground, beginning a spring that might offer water for the metropolis, even as moreover bearing a promise that Athens will be exceptional as a naval power. Athena, but, created the olive tree, the mainstay in their economic gadget, for the Athenians, which moreover symbolized peace, alternate and prosperity. The Athenians decided on the latter, and for this reason named their town Athens. The olive tree which Athena had seeded supposedly grew atop the Acropolis in a sacred enclosure, in which it have become purported to but be fame until it have become destroyed via way of the Persians for the duration of the sack of Athens within the wake of the incredible warfare at Thermopylae. Supposedly, however, a glowing shoot sprung from the burnt and broken carcass of the tree.

Chapter 2: A replica of Phidias's statue depicting Athena

Mythology apart, archaeological proof indicates that Athens changed into inhabited no much less than from the Neolithic Age, likely from among 5000-4000 BCE, making it one of the oldest identified constantly inhabited towns. It is straightforward to see why it turn out to be this type of right region; the rocky scarp which later have end up the political and spiritual middle of Classical Athens, the Acropolis, is a superb natural protecting position, watered with the aid of the Eridanus river at its foot and exceedingly tough to climb if a determined enemy is ready to contest the heights. It also gives a 360 diploma view of the flat, fertile plains surrounding it. The Cephisian undeniable, because it have become diagnosed, modified into additionally remarkably properly-irrigated, a need in the course of the baking Greek summers, and in factor bordered via the usage of using mountains, Pentelicus and Himmetus. Immediately to the west, about 3 miles away, the rocky promontory of the Piraeus jutted out to sea, developing the dual bays of Piraeus and Phaleron, herbal harbors a stone's throw away which have been to play a big function inside the next improvement of Athens.

This first-class geographical situation meant that Athens prospered, speedy growing from a few scattered huts inhabiting the herbal protective feature of the Acropolis proper right into a giant agreement. During the Golden Age of Mycenae, Athens became one of the maximum outstanding cities in Hellas, and there is enough archaeological proof to useful resource this. Though Athens honestly alternatively affords no outstanding heroes to fight in competition to Troy in Homer's Iliad, the stays of ancient foundations and homes indicate that the Mycenaean generation was one in each of undoubted increase for the town. The remains of a massive Mycenean fortification atop the Acropolis, dated round 1400 BCE, suggest that the metropolis's population had, at the least, sufficient wealth to make it profitable to collect a castle and curtain partitions round their most crucial defensive outpost.

The Acropolis modified into also the net net web page of a sprawling palatial complex, even though little remains of it in recent times except its foundations, and someday spherical 1200 BCE the fortress modified into made even extra formidable with the beneficial aid of the addition of a carved stone staircase, chiseled from the bare face of the Acropolis's rock, which led right proper down to a sheltered spring, as a end result allowing the fort to have its very personal water supply. The manufacturing of this staircase may additionally moreover have had something to do with the fabled Dorian Invasion, the quasi-legendary event which, someday round 1200 BCE, is stated to have delivered the Mycenean civilization low. It is unsure whether or now not or no longer the Dorians have been an invading, external strain or a downtrodden majority already gift on Greek soil, but their ascendancy modified into marked thru a period of tumult and social decline for Greece, one which Athens appears to have been, with the resource of all debts, spared. Unlike their longtime competitors the Spartans, the Athenians claimed no Doric descent, mentioning alternatively their natural Ionian lineage, suggesting that the Dorian Invasion largely surpassed them by means of, likely because of the Acropolis's ambitious natural defences. Whatever the motive, although it modified into spared the ravages of war Athens additionally seems to have suffered. Though it is unsure whether or not or now not there was a specific population drop inside the wake of the Invasion, the shortage of any crucial facilities left to exchange with in Greece possibly took its toll, and Athens went right into a decline that lasted nearly centuries.

However, archaeological proof from Iron Age internet sites across Attica (Athens' heartland) appears to signify that, via way of 900 BCE, Athens have end up one of the pre-eminent towns in all of Hellas, due to the mixture of her unassailable fortified metropolis-middle and her proximity to considered one of Greece's excellent natural harbors, a double advantage which modified into denied to the opportunity notable poleis, which can generally boast one or the alternative (Thebes and Sparta had impregnable heartlands, even as Corinth had a nice harbor). This Athenian ascendancy delivered on a protracted method of assimilation, referred to as synoikismos, or "forging into one residence". Synoikismos lasted approximately centuries and does not seem to had been characterized through using an excessive diploma of violence – as an alternative, the poleis round Athens appear to have meekly turn out to be assimilated into the complete. By the 7th century BCE, all of Attica modified into under direct Athenian control and manipulate, developing one of the most powerful metropolis-states in Greece.

It appears – although information are in reality nonexistent – that in this period Athens changed into no longer ruled via Kings and had already taken the first step closer to democracy via accomplishing a species of oligarchy. According to way of life, the Kings of Athens, who had held sway due to the fact round 1500 BCE, ended their line with Codrus, who end up said to have repelled an invasion through the usage of way of the Dorians spherical one thousand BCE, and whose descendants thereafter took at the feature of Archon in desire to King (despite the fact that the Archonship have come to be even though hereditary for nearly 3 centuries, its strength was not as absolute as that of the Kings). The Archons have been assisted of their rule with the aid of the eupatridae ("nobly-birthed") contributors, who have been elected to the council of the Aeropagus, which would possibly later end up an important political organ in Classical Athens. The Aeropagus, which have end up named after the hill sacred to Ares, God of War, wherein it met, became answerable for the election of the Polemarch ("warlord") who modified into answerable for army topics, and a number of unique minor Archons later formalized as nine.

Though a social hierarchy existed, it had no longer but obtained the weight of tradition and codification, and man or woman political and social rights had been in big part a query of what tribe the man or woman belonged to. If he became a member of one of the four primary tribes whose synoikismos had given shipping to Athens right, then a citizen of Athens must anticipate a first-rate diploma of freedom: he can also moreover want to induct (or "undertake") someone into his tribe, thereby extending those rights to him; he have to worship whoever he decided on;

he had the right to be buried on tribal land; he have to inherit his forebears' patrimony, in addition to a say within the election of the Archons and different political figures; and he had the usage of common tribal belongings. On the possibility hand, girls had no political rights and couldn't inherit, nor ought to men marry internal their very private tribe until a lady of the tribe have become widowed and her circle of relatives had to preserve the dowry in her circle of relatives.

The rule of the eupatridae, however, brought about unavoidable outcomes: a large, downtrodden and politically unrepresented personnel started out out to seethe with discontent, and via the use of manner of spherical 650 BCE topics had come to a head with social unrest rife inside the path of Attica. Unlike the Spartans, who determined on to reply social unrest with repression, the Athenians chose a one in each of a type, much much less-trodden path: reform. Under the auspices of Draco the Law-Giver, a modern-day charter have come to be drafted and (for the primary time) immortalized in writing, to save you abuse by using way of the keepers of the oral lifestyle. The Draconian code became strict – therefore the adoption of the time period in current English – however in massive component honest: murderers were sentenced to loss of existence, those responsible of manslaughter to exile, and borrowers want to face slavery if their creditor have become greater aristocratic than they had been. However, the introduction of the shortage of existence penalty for a number of minor crimes proved to be politically risky and unsuccessful.

Thus, in the wake of the Draconian reforms, which came about round 620 BCE, the terrific legislator Solon took over the tries at reform in 594 BCE. All Draco's felony suggestions, save for the ones punishing and distinguishing homicide and manslaughter, were repealed, and the charter changed into redrafted with a watch to social equality. The male population of Athens emerge as divided into four social lessons, based absolutely mostly on wealth and taxable assets represented with the useful resource of sacks of grain. The pentacosiomedimnoi must serve as strageoi, or generals. The Hippeis, or knights, may also additionally want to combat as cavalry squaddies (a whole lot tons less useful in Greek warfare however historically greater aristocratic than their infantry brethren, the hoplites). Then came the zeugitai, or hoplites, and the Thetai, or running schooling, who typically achieved their military provider as volunteer rowers inside the fleet. Although best pentacosiomedimnoi had been eligible for the archonship and membership of the Aeropagus, all one-of-a-kind residents (collectively with, for the primary time, the Thetai) must sit down at the Ecclesia, an administrative and judicial frame which held the archons and the Aeropagus accountable.

Aside from sowing the seeds of Athenian democracy, Solon's reforms went a step in addition via manner of assisting steer Athens a long way from its in large part subsistence-based totally completely agriculture and into the nascent business location. Though economic machine seems to have remained barter-primarily based definitely sincerely till approximately 50 years after Solon's reforms, Solon advocated the cultivation and export of olives, even as forbidding that of different, essential foodstuffs.

Solon introduced new, standardized weights and measures, granted citizenship to professional remote places tradesmen and craftsmen who emigrated to Athens, and in the long run ordered fathers to find out their sons a procedure or chance not having the proper to their sons' assist of their vintage age. Solon additionally placed a proper away save you to the enslavement of Athenian citizens because of debt, despite the fact that foreign places slaves though existed. In brief, Solon had sown the seeds for Athens's future supremacy. Economic reform and a resurgent, politically involved decrease beauty supposed that Athens prospered, and despite the fact that it could face extra setbacks within the destiny years, the direction for greatness grow to be set.

Chapter 3: Bust of Solon

The Persian Wars and the Start of the Golden Age of Athens

Sometime among six hundred and 550 BCE, Sparta grow to be though led through kings Agasicles and Leon, but with the useful resource of this aspect the Ephorate, a council of five elders, one from every deme of Sparta and with a big percent of the government strength, had additionally been brought. It changed into moreover round this time that Sparta waged a vicious war in the direction of the neighbouring city of Tegea, every different Arcadian polis. Tegea resisted with unparalleled tenacity, even causing a excessive defeat upon the Spartans at what have end up referred to as the Battle of the Fetters, and in the end Sparta turned into forced – in a sea-trade of coverage – to desist from its attempts to subjugate the Tegeans and reduce them to helot recognition. Sparta as a substitute everyday a grudging settlement from the Tegeans to accept Sparta as their hegemon (overlord). This stubborn resistance led the Tegeans to accumulate a vast amount of popularity as warriors, their valour and potential at palms being characterised by way of the usage of manner of historical Greek historians as being 2d excellent to that of the Spartans themselves.

The upshot of the conflict turned into that Sparta now won a valuable brilliant friend in ensuring the persevering with pacification of the pressured Messenian territory, and additionally a buffer amongst its very own dominions and people of the closest rival superpower, the terrific town of Argos. The following a long time of Spartan insurance had been to be shaped via the use of their desire to gain ascendancy over Argos, and in 546 BCE, following the Battle of Champions, Sparta inflicted every other crucial reversal on the Argives through taking control of the no-man's-land of Cynuria. Cynuria were a contested territory which stood amongst Argolis, the Argive sphere of effect, and Laconia, the fledgling Spartan Peloponnesian area (therefore the modern-day word "laconic", due to the fact the Spartans have been notorious for being men of few phrases).

Approximately half of of a century after the Battle of Champions, in 494 BCE Sparta released a robust excursion under King Cleomenes with the goal of destroying Argos as fast as and for all. The Argives fought lower returned, but their forces had been annihilated through way of the Spartan heavy infantry on the Battle of Sepeia, causing such devastation to the Argive war attempt that they correctly became a 2nd-price electricity. The Argives have been forced to acquiesce to humiliating peace phrases. It is said that after Cleomenes become asked why he had spared Argos whilst it lay prostrated and defenceless in advance than him, he remarked mildly that Sparta needed the Argives – they gave young Spartans a few issue to workout on.

The defeat of Argos installed Sparta as soon as and for all due to the fact the dominant land energy at some stage in all of Hellas, its armies invincible and its might in all likelihood unquestioned. Other powers, especially Athens, is probably greater dominant at sea, but anywhere war modified into joined on land, the Spartans were with out peer. As Sparta abruptly vaulted into ascendancy, envoys poured in from as some distance afield as Scythia and Lydia soliciting for Spartan useful resource in opposition to the Persian Emperor Darius, whose ruthless expansionist coverage was poised to threaten half of the identified worldwide, collectively with Greece herself, for whom Sparta had taken upon itself the self-appointed feature of champion.

Closer to domestic, the towns of the Ionian seaboard (Middle-Eastern in terms of geographic vicinity, but Greek in ethnic historical past and lifestyle) begged for help of their rise up closer to Darius, at the identical time due to the fact the Greek towns of Megara and Plataea, and later Corinth, declared their loyalty to Sparta, setting up the beginnings of what later have become called the Peloponnesian League. The League, that can in the end come to be one of the great political forces in ancient Greece, did now not get off to the maximum a hit of begins offevolved offevolved. The first joint attempt with the useful resource of the Peloponnesian League, and the primary time Sparta had attempted to mention its political supremacy north of the Isthmus of Corinth, got here whilst the 2 Spartan kings Cleomenes and Demaratos led an excursion into Attica, Athens's heartland. The Spartans had helped overthrow the Athenian ruler Hippias hastily earlier than, in 510 BCE, and with political activities, headed thru Cleisthenes and Isagoras respectively, vying for supremacy, the situation seemed ripe for political exploitation. The Spartans attempted to all over again the conservative Isagoras, however the tour modified into an entire fiasco: the allies, apprised of the Spartans' intentions, decamped en masse, and then the Spartan army itself become riven in while Demaratos quarrelled with Cleomenes and determined to up the stakes and bypass lower returned home as properly. As a end result, Spartan credibility changed into pretty damaged; in region of being uncontested leaders of the Peloponnesian League, they have been now expected to defer to their allies even as it came to selection-making, leaving them as a number one amongst equals instead of the overlords they could have in all likelihood desired to be. (As an interesting apart, Demaratos could later be exiled and wound up searching the Battle of Thermopylae from Xerxes's tent.

The league itself stood employer, but its goal appears to have shifted. Rather than ensuring Spartan supremacy, it changed into now geared toward resisting outside intervention. Cleomenes, it appears, had scented a change inside the wind. For loads of years, Greece had been riven with factionalism and inner strife, but the time have come to be abruptly drawing close to while all such variations want to be set apart. The could probable of the Persian empire, the fine the area had ever visible, became being massed in competition to them thru the Emperor Darius. The Persian empire used its unbelievable wealth to equip an army whose numbers have been so massive they defied knowledge. In truth, it's predicted that each province of Persia changed into able to elevating more men than all of the Greek poleis blended.

Ancient Greek depiction of the Persian Emperor Darius

As Sparta have been setting up itself, the Athenian Solon had set the extent for the beginning of the area's first recorded democracy, but it is doubtful what his reasons were, or his strategies. Though he allowed the Thetai political rights thru giving them the energy to sit in the Ecclesia and freed them from the regular fear of debt-added about bondage, Solon additionally switched the number one agricultural manufacturing from grain to olives, and at the same time as grain modified proper right into a subsistence crop it as a minimum gave the Thetai some element to subsist on, at the identical time as olives did now not (similarly they took severa years to start bearing fruit, and people years can't were smooth for the agricultural negative. It is unclear whether or no longer Solon fed them on the treasury's value).

Sea-primarily based exchange had additionally been at the wane in Athens over the previous years, due to a war with Megara, whose ships controlled the seas spherical nearby Salamis and Eulesis. The Megarans were ultimately defeated, contemplating a miles improved influx of change, by means of the usage of Solon's cousin, Peisistratos in 565 BCE Peisistratos changed into a few detail of a populist, and the use of excessive on the fulfillment of his task in the direction of the Megarans, he had interests of high place of job. However, he could not choice to gather his political development primarily based mostly on his recognition as a strategos by myself, so round 560 BCE he faked an strive on his life after which went in advance than the Ecclesia to call for bodyguards. Once he had the men, he used them to seize control of the Acropolis and set himself up as a tyrannos – a form of benevolent dictator. Despite the fact that Peisistratos had seized strength by means of manner of pressure, he was extraordinarily properly-regarded in Athens and persevered Solon's culture by way of using manner of increasing Athens's buying and selling and military affect in the Aegean, and promoting the development of schools of philosophy, technological information and the humanities. He furthermore observed out that Athenian predominance trusted naval might likely, a key thing in later Athenian politics.

Peisistratos had a rocky time in office and have become even exiled two times, but he managed to essentially hold onto energy till his loss of life in 527 BCE Peisistratos's call end up no longer speculated to be hereditary, however his sons Hippias and Hipparchus took strength no matter the dreams of most of the population, until Hipparchus became murdered in 514 BCE and Hippias set himself up as a despot. He became sooner or later overthrown in 510 BCE, at which factor authorities was handed to the aristocrat Cleisthenes, who in his time in office set up the definitive Athenian democratic political tool. He abolished the 4 tribes, or philai, whose synoikismos had first made Athens, and created ten non-elegance-based totally totally virtually ones, that have been in flip divided into 3 trittias, each of which modified into chargeable for one (or several) demes, which served as a species of neighbourhood council. Each of the philai furnished 50 elected representatives to the Boule, which have end up the number one governing body of the city. Public places of work have emerge as lottery-based, keep for the ten strategoi, in which it modified into glaringly felt that chance have emerge as a awful way of choosing a desired.

Athens now emerged a number of the poleis of Hellas as a dynamic and bold strain, each politically and militarily. The Spartans, who up until that 2d have been the uncontested top canine in Greece, started to sit up and take phrase. In the wake of the exile of Hippias, who fled to Persia, the Spartans succeeded in putting in place a pro-Spartan oligarchy in Athens, marginalizing Cleisthenes or even having him exiled, but the populace of Athens rose up and expelled the pro-Spartan oligarchs, staying defiant even supposing the Spartans marched on Athens in what ultimately have become a navy debacle for the them. It regarded as although no longer some component may moreover need to stop the march to fulfillment of Athens and her new, radical political system.

However, barely a decade after the reforms of Cleisthenes consolidated the way of democratization set in movement through Draco and furthered with the aid of Solon, the touchy check of democracy risked being snuffed out altogether. Flushed with its dynamic upward push to incidence most of the towns of Hellas, in 499 BCE Athens overreached itself by way of responding to a name for help from the poleis of Ionia in Asia Minor. Though middle-japanese in geographical location, the Ionians have been ethnically and culturally Greek, and they been chafing below the rule of thumb of Darius of Persia. The Ionians, rebuffed with the aid of manner of Sparta, grew to turn out to be to Athens for help in their rise up.

Athens had recently prolonged long gone so far as to provide earth and water in submission to Persia when they had been at odds with Sparta, in go back for the promise of assistance, however they finally reversed their insurance even as the Persians insisted they allow Hippias to resume his place as tyrant. Thus, the Athenian fleet sailed in manual of the Ionians, most important to warfare with Persia.

In 491 BCE, following a a success invasion of Thrace over the Hellespont, Darius sent envoys to the primary Greek metropolis-states, which include Sparta and Athens, traumatic tokens of earth and water as symbols of submission. Darius didn't precisely get the answer he have become seeking out. According to Herodotus in his well-known Histories, "Xerxes however had not sent to Athens or to Sparta heralds to name for the present of earth, and because of this, mainly due to the fact on the previous time at the identical time as Dareios had despatched for this very reason, the simplest humans threw the guys who made the decision for into the pit and the others right right into a properly, and bade them take from thence earth and water and undergo them to the king."

Thus, in 490 BCE, after the rise up in Ionia had been overwhelmed, Darius despatched his large Mardonius, on the pinnacle of a large fleet and invading pressure, to break the meddlesome Greeks, beginning with Athens.

The Persian army, numbering everywhere among 30,000 and three hundred,000 men, landed on the obvious at Marathon, a few dozen miles from Athens, wherein an Athenian navy of 10,000 hoplite heavy infantry supported with the beneficial resource of 1,000 Plataeans organized to contest their passage. The Athenians appealed to the Spartans for help, but the Spartans dithered; regular with the Laws of Lycurgus, they had been forbidden to march till the waxing moon have become complete. Accordingly, their army arrived too overdue. Thus, it fell upon the Athenians to shoulder the load. With their military led by means of using the use of the extraordinary generals Miltiades and Themistocles, the Athenians charged the outnumbering Persians. Outmatched with the useful useful resource of the might likely of the heavy, bronze-armored Greek phalanx, the inferior Persian infantry have come to be enveloped and destroyed, inflicting them to interrupt out for their ships in panic. The Athenians had obtained a big victory in competition to an great and seemingly invincible enemy.

Chapter 4: Bust of Themistocles

According to legend, within the aftermath of Marathon one of the Greek infantrymen, already war-weary, named Pheidippides, ran the 26.2 miles lower again to Athens at the manner to announce the victory and collapsed and died as quick as he had completed so, primary to the popularity quo of the marathon in reminiscence of that feat inside the cutting-edge Olympics. The struggle has every other, an awful lot less inspiring aftermath, however. The yr after Marathon, in 489 BCE, an day adventure under Miltiades turned into launched in opposition to the Greek traitors at Paros. The day revel in became a failure and, in what could grow to be one in each of Athens's a good buy much less charming traditions, the hero of the hour emerge as have become the villain by demagogues who discovered out the energy of an infected mob inside the new democratic device; Miltiades, wounded and struggling, changed into sentenced to loss of life and thrown into prison, wherein he died of his wounds.

Despite the victory inside the First Persian War, it modified into felt that, likely no longer inside the next 365 days or maybe in the subsequent decade, the Persians must come over again. The Spartan king Leonidas modified into the principle advise of this concept, maintaining it even if Darius died and became succeeded by using the use of his son Xerxes in 486 BCE. Under Leonidas and their different king, Agesilaus, the Spartans waged a series of campaigns within the years following the Battle of Marathon to supply reluctant allies and Persian sympathizers into the fold and ensure a united Greek the the front could probably greet all Persian tries to invade.

That invasion, just as Leonidas had prophesied, got here in 480 BCE, even as Xerxes, on the pinnacle of an military which Herodotus states numbered over a million men, bridged the Hellespont (the Dardanelles straits) thru a massive pontoon bridge and marched his army into Thrace, threatening Greece right. All eyes grew to come to be to the Spartans: the best warriors in all of Greece, sincerely, want to guide the defence of Hellas. Yet once more, the Spartans dithered. It is unsure what introduced about the Spartan reluctance to take the sector. Some historians have endorsed that, being specifically concerned with the Peloponnese, the Spartans wanted to defend the Isthmus of Corinth, and allow the rest of Greece fend for itself. Others take transport of the authentic Spartan reason that as a deeply non secular human beings they could not forget about approximately the Olympic proscription, in electricity at that particular time of 12 months, that forbade Greek towns from marching in palms.

Whatever the motive, the Spartans may want to problem simplest a token strain: as a end result, they sent an "all-sire" suicide unit of three hundred full Spartiates, notionally the King's bodyguard, under Leonidas, to defend the pass at Thermopylae in north-japanese Greece. These three hundred had been bolstered with the aid of six hundred perioikoi or "friends" (truly "the ones close by"), line infantry of lesser reputation from the cities surrounding Sparta, and a similarly 900 helot slight soldiers, one for each hoplite. They had been also joined with the useful resource of amongst 3,000-5,000 thousand allied Greeks from Corinth, Arcadia, Mantinea, Tegea, Thespiae, Phokis, Locris, and others.

For three days, Leonidas, his Three Hundred, and their allies withstood wave upon wave of Persian assaults, inflicting extra than 20,000 casualties upon the enemy. Finally, outflanked and exhausted, they had been defeated; Leonidas despatched all of the allies in retreat shop for the remnant of the Three Hundred, but the Thespian infantrymen refused to head away, taking on their locations beside the Three Hundred. According to Herodotus, in the course of their mythical final stand, after their weapons and armor had been smashed and broken the Greeks fought on with nails and teeth before being at very last reduce all the way all of the way right

down to the ultimate man.

View of the bypass at Thermopylae. At the time of the warfare, the shoreline modified into form of wherein the street is in recent times, and the bushes on the left element of the picture could maximum in all likelihood were absent.

The great of Spartan valor, already considered legendary, now have grow to be eternal. When the Spartans' famous and sacrificial stand at Thermopylae ended, the Athenian fleet grow to be forced to fall yet again, and Xerxes's navy marched unopposed into Hellas in advance than advancing on Athens. The Greek armies had been scattered and now not able to face the may in all likelihood of Persia, so Athens changed into pressured to do the unthinkable: evacuate the entire population of the town to Salamis, from in which the Athenians watched in horror as Xerxes' troops plundered the defenceless city, set it aflame, and razed the Acropolis. However, the Athenians remained belligerent. According to the oracle at Delphi, "outstanding the wood wall shall save you", and this proved real while Themistocles managed to entice the Persian fleet into the straits of Salamis and there, with the Athenians within the lead, the allied Greek military annihilated the Persian fleet. Despite friction with the Spartans over which part of Greece need to be defended, and a similarly evacuation of Athens, in August 479 BCE a big allied Greek host succeeded in bringing Xerxes's considerable Mardonius's army to struggle at Plataea, in crucial Greece.

The Greeks had 50,000 guys, and the backbone of this pressure, below Pausanias, have been 5,000 complete Spartiates and five,000 perioikoi. In the ensuing conflict, the Persian forces were actually annihilated, and even though this had been a united Greek attempt, the credit score rating for the victory changed into placed firmly on Sparta's doorstep. Their ascendancy have become in addition confirmed later that equal one year at the same time as, in the end of the naval engagement at Mycale, the Hellenic army (commanded via the Spartan king Leotychides) grow to be answerable for the victory that finally scoured the Persian navy from the seas, a triumph which threatened to difficult to recognize the Athenian triumph at Salamis earlier in the war.

However, in the aftermath of Mycale, Sparta modified into absolutely though conflicted about pursuing expansionism outside of the Peloponnese and Greece itself. Thus, they grew to end up down overtures from the Ionian cities for assist of their renewed upward thrust up in opposition to Xerxes, rudely suggesting that they abandon their towns en masse and resettle in Greece, wherein space could be made for them via uprooting pro-Persian traitors. The Ionians, disgusted, refused to assist Pausanias (now in the role of navarch, or admiral) in his expeditions toward Byzantium and Cyprus and as a substitute grew to emerge as to Athens for help, which the seafaring power modified into thrilled to offer. The seeds of Athenian and Spartan competition, seeds that could eventually blossom into the worst struggle in Greece's information, have been sown.

The Athenians, through way of way of assessment, were thinking huge. Over the following decade they spearheaded a number of naval movements in opposition to Persian-held settlements and fortresses inside the Aegean, in addition growing Athens's have an effect on and laying the concept for what can also later come to be the Athenian empire. During this era the Athenian fleet, already pre-eminent, elevated and grew in enjoy and potential until it become the most effective naval force in all of the Mediterranean.

It grow to be for the duration of this period that Athens installation the Delian League; to start with predicted as a league of like-minded poleis with Athens performing as first among equals, but it quick degenerated right right into a situation in which unique cities had been essentially vassals of Athens. Meanwhile, the Spartans had commenced to broaden increasingly concerned about Athens's imperialistic hobbies and involved that their function of pre-eminence some of the Greeks ought to quickly be subverted. A disaster, it regarded, become inevitable.

Chapter 5: Greek Architecture

Christophe Meneboeuf's photo of the Acropolis in Athens

Perhaps the most characteristic characteristic of historic Greek shape is the manner in which houses were constructed. They had been composed of upright columns supporting horizontal beams all lintels helping a ridged roof. Originally those structures would have been composed of wood, however the first rate homes people though apprehend nowadays were fabricated from stone. The classical columns had been made up of a number of stone drums which rested one upon some other without mortar, despite the fact that in many systems a huge bronze pin ran thru them. The columns tapered from bottom to pinnacle and had been surmounted thru capitals.

There are 5 orders or sorts of columns based totally mostly on generation and vicinity. The Doric column changed into fluted and is the earliest example of Greek architectural fashion. The Ionic fashion originated inside the Asian Greek colonies inside the middle of the sixth century BCE and grow to be thinner than the Dorian, with scrolled capitals and assisting ornate friezes. Corinthian columns have been comparable, with the capitals elaborately embellished with scrolls and acanthi. The oldest stated shape in his fashion is the Choragic Monument of Lysicrates, a rich Roman citizen, built round 335 BCE. These four architectural styles long-established the premise of Roman, and therefore

European, shape and it's miles hard not to peer their impact in any metropolis or city in recent times.

Most public houses, especially temples, had been built of marble, or, in which this proved impractical, of limestone with a veneer of marble dust. Marble is more malleable than many styles of stone, and furthermore, it's miles lightly translucent, so its beauty is stronger within the mild. Marble also assumes one-of-a-type colorings, collectively with purple, white, green or yellow.

City-states that used marble in building public houses had been showing the wealth and grandeur of the metropolis. Marble came to be appeared as the noblest of constructing materials, expressing the divine and the proper. Even nowadays marble is considered one of the most valuable building materials, or even marble finishes are frequently used wherein real marble isn't.

The Acropolis, which certainly manner "a city on the heights," is a fort whose presently surviving systems have been widely speaking built in some unspecified time in the future of the fifth century BCE. In honor of Athena, the customer goddess of Athens. It functioned as a sacred precinct that contained the metropolis's maximum vital non secular and municipal structures, numerous which have remained extensively intact for over 2,000 years. The Propylaea (the gateway to the Acropolis), the Parthenon (the most shrine to the goddess), the Erechtheion (a shrine that supposedly homes the burial grounds of mythical Athenian kings), and the Temple of Athena Nike all live directly to this contemporary, and for the ones motives, the Acropolis is possibly the definitive and most eloquent expression of classical structure, if not of the classical form itself.

Naturally, like many particular works of its type and affect, the structures on the Acropolis embody first-class traditions, however additionally they cross away from a few traditions and additionally converted others. Indeed, surely because of the truth the Acropolis is Athens' maximum putting function, it is also an outstanding representative of the city's golden age, each in terms of classical style and civilization as an entire. It's no wonder that human beings maintain to view the Acropolis as both a portal to antiquity however additionally an opening with residing systems whose importance keeps to reverberate to nowadays.

The architectural complex at the Athenian Acropolis is universally acclaimed as one of the maximum high-quality achievements of Western Civilization, however indoors that group of iconic houses there may be absolute confidence that the Parthenon is the most well-known and notable. The Doric and Ionic paperwork that are the concept of classical form, and as implemented to the Parthenon, nonetheless resonate within the modern worldwide these days, as it has accomplished in the direction of the centuries thinking about the reality that its very last touch. It modified into built to the exceptional feasible necessities at the time, and no price turned into spared on every the constituent components or its ornament.

Of course, given the care and the expenses, people have always at a loss for words why the Athenians located a lot treasure and try into the improvement of this masterpiece, and why the temple though has such an impact on folks who see it nowadays. To truely recognize this most lovely and subtle of houses it's far essential to contextualize its manufacturing and its use inside the Athenian religious subculture. The Parthenon need to be seen from severa perspectives, such as its ancient context, its mathematical sophistication, and the myths and legends knowledgeable in its sculptures and friezes. Ultimately, but, the Parthenon wishes to be mentioned for what it changed into on the time, now not nice as an area of worship but a party of a momentous victory over a strong overseas strength, associated with a conscious glorification of Athens as a "cosmopolis". There is not any ambiguity; the temple have end up the planned articulation of Pericles' vision of Athens at the height of all its glory.

Originally a walled palace, the Parthenon have turn out to be a temple to the goddess of Athena, the titular god of the town. The first temple changed into constructed inside the Dorian style among 550 and 570 BCE. It become torn down and rebuilt instances earlier than being destroyed by way of The Persian King Xerxes in 480 BCE. The temple whose ruins stand nowadays modified into constructed after the Persians had been defeated. It housed a 9-meter excessive gold and ivory statue of Athena.

The gift Parthenon modified into built inside the Doric fashion, with 17 columns at the perimeters and eight at the façade. There have been 23 columns in the cella or internal temple, surrounding the statue of

Athena in levels. Six columns marked the entrance to the internal courtroom. Behind the statue were the treasury and four extremely good columns, differing from the rest in that they have been within the Ionic style, at the same time as the others have been Doric.

Leo von Klenze's painting of the Acropolis

(1846)

An 1893 image of the Acropolis displaying the Beulé Gate, Propylaea, and the Temple of Athena Nike

As a chunk of paintings, the Parthenon is terrific, but it's also a technological marvel.

The temple changed into built without the use of right now traces, and the columns narrow slightly from pinnacle to bottom and curve inwards towards the top as although they have been struggling to endure the weight of the roof. There are other diffused talents contained within the shape of the Parthenon, together with the fact that the architects adjusted the width of the outer nook columns that allows you to make amends for the brightness of mild which might also otherwise reason them to seem in addition aside than they in reality are. Everything about the Parthenon presentations the Greeks' obsession approximately human artifice due to the fact the idealization of nature.

A project to restore the Parthenon to its genuine glory, funded via the Greek Republic and the European Union, started out in 1975 and has exposed some startling developments of Greek shape. Its resilience is especially noteworthy, considering that a incredible many temples and specific public homes had been constructed on pinnacle of hilltops in areas mentioned for seismic interest. Indeed, architects and archaeologists are reading the Parthenon to look at the way it has withstood multiple earthquakes at some point of its 2,4 hundred 12 months facts. As these days as 1999, a five.Nine Richter scale earthquake killed 143 human beings in the region of Athens, however it left the Parthenon almost really intact.

The Parthenon is constructed on a limestone basis 12 meters underneath the floor and the columns, it is to be remembered, aren't positive via mortar. The blocks applied in its manufacturing had been joined thru H-fashioned iron pins that have been covered with lead so as no longer to corrode. However, stabilizing pins inserted within the 19th century were no longer so included and had corroded by the point recovery started out out. It is a surprise then that a ruined temple need to have withstood the rigors of an active earthquake place, lots simply so scientist and engineers from earthquake-stricken Japan have journeyed to Athens to have a take a look at the building.

Initial research have indicated that the temple's resilience might also moreover moreover have some aspect to do with how the columns are built. Further, the truth that the Parthenon modified into constructed with out mortar may additionally additionally have given the form positive flexibility while an earthquake struck. More research are wanted, and engineering professionals accept as true with the extraordinary Parthenon has more secrets and techniques to reveal.

In its entire glory, the Parthenon ought to have been approximately forty five feet immoderate, a hundred feet huge, and over 2 hundred toes extended. It took at least 8 years to collect, an brilliant quantity of time considering the workmanship concerned and the perfection of the completed form.

Other monuments to Greek architectural genius which include the Temple of Zeus at Olympia completed in 457 BCE. Long for the reason that destroyed, it housed a statue of Zeus enthroned about 45 toes immoderate and, much like the statue of Athena, labored in gold and ivory. Ivory have emerge as a commonplace material used for sculpture in the historical global, and its aggregate with gold turn out to be a completely famous and archaic shape of statuary referred to as "chryselephantine" that modified into generally used for outsized cult statues, perhaps as it come to be specifically moderate as compared to stone. The statue of Zeus portrayed Zeus seated on a jewel-inlaid throne, probable in a function similar to the famous statue of Abraham Lincoln inside the Lincoln Memorial in Washington, D.C. It emerge as additionally recommended that Zeus held a small statue of Nike (the Greek goddess of Victory) in his right hand and a gold-inlaid employees, topped with a gold eagle, in his left.

A temple have become constructed simply to house the statue, and a few said that it modified into lit with the aid of fireside within the windowless temple, making the statue of Zeus a mysterious and enforcing sight. To get an concept of truly how large and imposing the statue itself have become, the historical historian Strabo wrote, "It seems that if Zeus have been to upward push up, he could probably unroof the temple." It inspired awe in others who saw it as nicely; Plutarch wrote in his Life of Paulus that when the Roman latest noticed the statue, he was "became moved to his soul, as even though he had visible the god in person." 1st century BCE Greek orator Dio Chrysostom said seeing the statue have to make a person forget about about all his problems.

The temple, together with the statue, became destroyed thru the Christian Emperor Theodosius II in 426 CE. The first-rate statue end up apparently constructed after which moved into the cella of the temple. In reality, the statue have end up so huge that the columns of the cella needed to be dismantled to position within the statue after which reassembled.

Other super architectural wonders of the Greek international embody the Temple of Artemis, the Mausoleum at Halicarnassus, the Colossus of Rhodes, and the Lighthouse of Alexandria. Of the seven super wonders of the Ancient World, 5 out of seven are merchandise of Greek civilization.

Drawing of Colossus of Rhodes, illustrated within the Grolier Society's 1911 Book of Knowledge

The Colossus of Rhodes come to be a statue of Helios, god of the sun, which stood about a hundred ft excessive at the doorway of the harbor of the island u . S . Of Rhodes. It changed into built through Chares of Lindos in 280 BCE as an imparting for the island's victory over Cyprus. The statue emerge as constructed of bronze and stood on a marble base about 50 feet immoderate.

The Colossus took 12 years to bring together, and earthen ramps had been raised at some stage in advent and made better due to the fact the statue grew. The ft have been carved in stone and protected in bronze plates riveted collectively. The ankles and legs had been framed in iron and moreover protected in bronze plates. Most of the plates of the lower body had been amongst 20 and 25 millimeters, at the same time as those of the higher frame may be thinner, among 6.6 and 12.Five millimeters.

Little is cited now approximately its actual look, collectively with whether or now not it became clothed, the coiffure, or maybe its posture, however it come to be dedicated to the solar god Helios. Some (lots later) snap shots of it show it protective aloft a fiery torch, similar to the Statue of Liberty, indicating it could furthermore have had a virtually practical reason of guiding ships into the harbor, which had a as an alternative slender mouth.

This amazing statue, unrivaled thru way of some thing else inside the historic worldwide, grow to be destroyed via an earthquake in 226 BCE, 54 years after it have end up completed. When the Colossus changed into completed, it emerge as committed, "To you, o Sun, the humans of Dorian Rhodes installation this bronze statue attaining to Olympus, once they had pacified the waves of battle and crowned their metropolis with the spoils taken from the enemy. Not satisfactory over the seas however also on land did they kindle the cute torch of freedom and independence. For to the descendants of Herakles belongs dominion over sea and land."

Given its layout, while the earthquake that knocked it down struck in 226 BCE, historians theorize that the plates shook free, arms first, and the statue fell in numerous portions, leaving the toes and the bottom status. There is likewise some debate as to its function and stance. Some medieval property claimed that it changed into constructed to straddle the harbor, as immortalized in Shakespeare's play, Julius Caesar. However, there are capacity issues with this photo. One is a case of balance, due to the fact the bronze statue would probable have fallen even greater fast than it did, below its non-public weight. Archaeologists additionally hold in mind that making the statue straddle the harbor should have required remaining the entire harbor at some point of its manufacturing, and the destruction of the statue could have blocked front to the harbor as well.

More proof suggesting the statue did now not straddle the harbor comes from eyewitness money owed approximately the stays of the statue, which incorporates that of historians Strabo and Pliny the Elder. Though the statue have end up felled through an earthquake inside the early 1/three century, quantities of it stayed wherein they had been for eight centuries, in element because the Rhodians did now not have the coronary coronary heart to break them down and in component because of the reality they had been in all likelihood too big to be moved. However, they have been said to be at the banks of the harbor. If the statue had straddled the harbor mouth, the falling portions would likely have choked the harbor and could have needed to be moved.

After an earthquake toppled the statue and devastated the metropolis in 226 BCE, the portions remained for pretty a long term earlier than they were in the end hauled off after the Muslim conquest of Rhodes. The eighth century CE Byzantine monk Theophanes Confessor claimed that the Muslim army provided off the quantities in 654 BCE to a "Jewish service issuer of Edessa," despite the fact that this tale may be a literary invention supposed to predict the upcoming Apocalypse. It is also feasible that the Knights of St. John, who held the island in the past due Middle Ages, broke down the portions and used the although-precious bronze for scrap. At any fee, no final quantities have now not all started been discovered in present day instances, so every the internet site and the arrival of the statue live a thriller. Some have even speculated that it in fact stood atop Rhodes' acropolis, now not at the mouth of the harbor.

Though it changed into ultimately too experimental to have survived lengthy, the Colossus turned into a terrific success for the Greeks and drew masses interest from Greek historians. Even those travelling after it had fallen had been struck with awe at the sight of the ruins, and the ruins themselves were a vacationer destination.

Pliny the Elder wrote that every of the statue's arms were huge than most statues. Not distinctly, the Colossus has lent its name through the passage of time as an outline for any massive item.

The Lighthouse or Pharos of Alexandria, constructed on the little island of that call, come to be another architectural wonder. It modified into commissioned with the aid of using the primary Greek King of Egypt, Ptolemy I (r.305 – 282) and took 12 years to build. Sostratus of Cnidus can also had been the architect. Fortunately, this extremely good shape survived into medieval times, and the Arab rulers of Egypt defined it in some detail. It grow to be described as being built of large, moderate-coloured stone blocks and crafted from 3 stages. The backside and relevant tower had 4 facets and tapered from bottom to pinnacle. It stood on a rectangular, walled platform. A hexagonal tower stood on the number one and a narrower, and a round tower on top of that. At the apex changed proper into a flame that burned through using manner of night time time time and a replicate that contemplated the moderate in the course of the day. A statue of Poseidon or likely Zeus surmounted the complete edifice, which stood over six hundred toes tall and had a base of approximately one hundred square toes.

The Pharos lighthouse end up now not the number one lighthouse to be built, but it did end up the version of all future lighthouses until the 18th century, lots just so Pharos have end up the etymological base of the word for a lighthouse in plenty of languages. This consists of the Greek phrase Pharos, the Persian word fanus, the Italian phrase faro, and the Bulgarian word a long way.

During the Middle Ages Lighthouse of Alexandria suffered from numerous earthquakes, and the final remnants of it disappeared in 1480 even as a fort become built at the website online. In 1994, archaeologists located remains of the lighthouse underneath the sea in Alexandria's harbor. As with the Colossus of Rhodes, some of proposals were advise to reconstruct the Lighthouse of Alexandria, however so far, no efforts had been made.

Chapter 6: Engineering

Given that the Greeks constructed architectural wonders, it's no surprise that their engineering modified into superior for the generation.

At first, the Greeks used the smooth technology of ramps to transport stone and precise substances vertically. However, round 515 BCE, there may be evidence that machines had been used for this purpose.

The invention of the winch and pulley induced the usage of cranes. The handiest crane come to be called the trispastos, which operated with the aid of way of three pulleys and had a one hundred fifty kilogram load. The crane had superb advantages over a ramp, specifically for a polis, because it required few guys to characteristic it, at the same time as a ramp required many slaves to haul material in place. Small metropolis-states did not typically have the capability to mobilize this form of personnel.

Over time, the way of production for that reason changed. Blocks tended to be smaller and columns have been constructed of smaller and additional plausible portions in vicinity of a monolith. Cranes had been later devised for handling heavy hundreds, which have been moved by way of way of way of fellows walking on a treadmill. In fact, masses of cranes have been built for one-of-a-kind goals, and they is probably moved with the useful resource of animals or thru way of fellows typically on wheels. The 4-mast crane have emerge as constructed of 4 vertical joists related to horizontal beams and changed into moved on rollers to in which it modified into wanted. Another kind of crane had winches on both element of a vertical frame. The lifting arm is probably turned around on its base, which made it suitable for loading and unloading ships and for the improvement of ports.

Other lifting mechanisms used by the Greeks blanketed the hoist, which used a pulley with as a lot as four reels. They additionally devised severa creative strategies of mooring rope in stone blocks for the skills of lifting them. Two horizontal grooves might be carved into the bottom to allow a doubled rope to be linked to a hook. Four equidistant holes may additionally furthermore be bored from pinnacle to bottom and the doubled rope threaded thru them. Another approach entailed carving four vertical grooves along the edges of the stone. The Greeks devised numerous bronze-articulated tongs or pincers that clung into carved grooves. Metal wedges in trapezoid sockets had been appreciably utilized to high-quality impact.

As admirable as the ones innovations were, the Greek use of hydraulic energy is in all likelihood the most beautiful in the minds of present day engineers. The kilonion, a drastically smooth device which include a horizontal beam with a bucket on one factor and a counterweight on the other, drew water from rivers, streams, and wells and changed into utilized by distinctive historical civilizations. In ancient Greece, this generation advanced into the hydraulic wheel, the number one evidence of that is to be determined at the excavations of Perachora Korinthias, which changed proper right into a sanctuary in honor of the goddess Hera ruled by using the polis of Corinth. Ruins right proper right here from the third millennium BCE recommend the presence of this historical water pump, which consisted of a massive wheel moved by way of manner of animals, at the side of an ox, rotating a small prolonged wheel, which in flip turned round some exclusive wheel that became the larger one. Water have become drawn in bronze or clay buckets and tipped proper right into a channel. Such a pump changed into used for irrigation features.

The 4th century BCE Athenian architect Philon designed a water pump consisting of a large radiated wheel positioned over a channel. A man striding on pinnacle drove the wheel, and embedded wood packing containers emptied water into wood channels. The identical architect also invented the mangani, a vertical chain of field suspended above a channel. It emptied water into an accelerated wooden channel and, in evaluation to the preceding pumps, end up pushed actually through the strain of the water itself.

The maximum famous ancient Greek pump is truly the Archimedes screw or screw pump. At its coronary coronary heart, the screw is a reasonably number one layout, but it's miles an stylish technique to an prolonged-lasting hassle: the want to switch water from above its stage. The historic international had devised a series of answers to this problem, from the development of aqueducts to the employment of bucket and pulley systems and water wheels, however aqueducts nonetheless flowed at least barely downhill and different structures had a restricted capacity. Archimedes sought to remedy this hassle with the development of the Screw. The mechanism emerge as a huge cylindrical screw, long-mounted in a whole lot the equal form as a commonplace wooden screw, sheathed inner a cylindrical receptacle. The screw gadget, which may both were built of wooden or of sheet steel, become grew to become counting on period by both a person the use of a lever or draught animals collectively with horses or oxen. The bottom cease of the screw might be positioned in the water, even as the top surrender could be the peak to which the water ought to be displaced to. The motion of turning the screw may slowly drift the water vertically, and at the same time as some water would possibly probably escape because of the reality the seal among the brink of the screw's "blades" and the cylinder containing it couldn't be watertight (for the purpose that otherwise the screw have to now not turn), the seepage modified into slight.

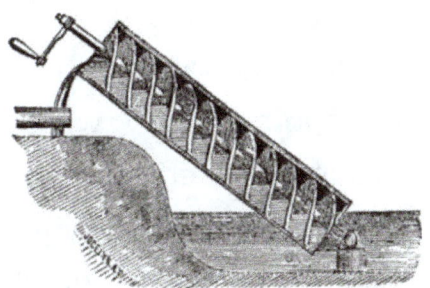

Illustration showing the characteristic of the screw

Some researchers have recommended that the historical Greeks were not the primary to apply the form of pump. For example, the archaeologist Stephanie Daly has recommended that the Assyrians used it inside the introduction of the Hanging Gardens of Babylon. However, despite the fact that this is the case, evidently it grow to be the Greeks who designed a tool that might be extensively disseminated.

The Greeks applied hydraulic generation to outstanding functions except irrigation. Hero of Alexandria (c.10 – c.70 AD) grow to be a fact seeker, mathematician, and engineer who invented a terrific many devices, and he appeared to were concerned approximately water and its possibilities in engineering. He built a dual suction strain piston pump with a pivoted lever. The tank moved on four wheels and end up used to fight fires. The identical genius who invented this contraption additionally designed an area pump which encompass a water-evidence metallic ball with a piston indoors that compressed air, inflicting water to spray out through a nozzle. It is simple to look how this tool can also moreover be beneficial in firefighting.

While not an engineering tool, the Pythagoras cup is likewise well really worth of factor out. This uncommon eating vessel is considered to be an invention of the sixth century BCE truth seeker Pythagoras, who purportedly used it to illustrate the virtues of moderation to his disciples. The steel cup had a siphon inside the center of it, and even as it changed into filled above the extent of the siphon all the liquid became tired via that siphon. The Pythagoras cup end up furthermore referred to as the cup of justice as it illustrated the outcomes of vengeance: punishment commensurate to the offense changed into justice. To the Greeks, excessive punishment changed into not only unfair however emptied the motion of justice surely. Cisterns in contemporary-day bathrooms feature upon the equal precept because the Pythagoras cup - while the water level reaches the top of the siphon the contents of the cistern drain away.

Military Technology

The historic Greek poleis had been built on natural defenses, together with hilltops or by rivers or circumscribed through sea. Moreover, they had been continuously defended thru metropolis walls. The earliest fortification could have been timber palisades which includes those noted through Homer inside the 8th century BCE, and the English word wall comes (via Latin) from the Greek phrase for "stake" or "post."

Several centuries later, the Greeks had been constructing complicated protecting walls manufactured from stone. The most famous of these walls were those of Athens, commenced after the Persians sacked Athens in 480 BCE. When rebuilding the wall, the Athenians had been aware that their essential power lay in its navy and mercantile fleet. Thus, now not best did they construct walls throughout the metropolis and spherical their port, Piraeus, but they constructed a fortified thoroughfare maximum of the two settlements, over a distance of 6 kilometers. This Long Wall made Athens nearly not feasible to conquer because of the fact, until the 4th century BCE, towns in historical Greek instances were notably speakme taken via starving the populace and forcing them to surrender. Greek armies did own and use siege engines, as may be defined under, however those not regularly took towns through themselves.

The Long Wall averted an military from surrounding Athens and decreasing its resources, and Piraeus couldn't be efficiently blockaded because of the scale and energy of the Athenian fleet. In the 440s the Athenians delivered a second wall connecting the metropolis and the port, at a time even as their naval power have become declining.

Siege technology changed into essential in the limitless wars a few of the Greek city-states. However, till the fifth century, the historical Greeks hardly ever engaged in the full-scale town assaults, preferring to depend upon the prowess in their infantrymen in pitched battles or skirmishes. The reliance on sieges modified in 399 BCE even as the Carthaginian general Himilco laid siege to the Greek town of Syracuse in Sicily. The Carthaginians surrounded the metropolis and its 30,000 defenders with 50,000 men.

The King of Syracuse, Dionysius, had made huge preparations for the siege, refortifying the wall that surrounded not most effective the isthmus upon which the precise city grow to be constructed however the suburbs at the mainland as nicely. He also constructed a seawall round a section of the harbor so you can guard his fleet. These systematized fortifications defeated the Carthaginian enemies.

Just a long term after the Siege of Syracuse, the Greeks have been devising a whole lot of battle engines for every defensive and offensive functions. The hovering ram emerge as one of the first guns designed for proper now assaulting the walls of a metropolis. It turn out to be specifically clean in manufacturing, together with a metallic-capped beam suspended in a body that end up drawn on wheels. The suspension allowed the beam to be thrust in competition to a stone structure at one in each of a type angles, the higher to take benefit of weaknesses. The gain of this device became that it became pretty moderate and easy to move. On the opportunity hand, however, it modified into unprotected from missile assaults and incendiary guns which include burning pitch.

In the 4th century BCE Alexander the Great's engineer, Diades of Pella (nicknamed "The Besieger" due to his prowess in designing siege machines), made a cellular ram that turn out to be in reality enclosed in a tent-fashioned timber casing with a fireplace-evidence pitched roof. At the the the front of the engine emerge as a three-story turret with domestic home windows in that have been placed archers and small catapults. The heavy ram turn out to be moved over cylindrical rollers and thrust via ropes.

Water became even saved within the engine to position out fires that might get away. The trypanon or "borer," additionally invented through Diades, emerge as a modification, and not the use of a turret and a ram moved with the aid of a winch and pulleys. Unlike a desired ram that tried to shatter stone, the trypanon had a pointed tip for penetrating walls.

Another device utilized by Diades modified into the tortoise, a wheeled cage with four padded partitions forming a pyramid. This contraption end up moved to defensive ditches, in which engineers inside it stuffed them in to allow siege engines which includes rams to approach the enemy's walls. The tortoise's safety consisted of steel plates, wickerwork, clay blended with hair, and lambskins complete of vinegar-soaked seaweed.

The paintings of the tortoise also can very well have preceded the approaching of the helepolis, an amazing engine invented thru Epimachos for the Siege of Rhodes in 305 BCE. The name helepolis technique "metropolis taker," and it became a siege tower 9 memories (forty one meters) immoderate. According to Diodorus, it changed into a siege tower with a square base of 50x50 cubits (approximately 75x75 toes), and it stood a complete of 9 reminiscences excessive. The tool have become framed from wood and iron, and grow to be hooked up on eight stable wheels covered in iron plates. Plates of iron additionally covered three of the 4 partitions of the device. Every story turn out to be packed with a large choice of engines to release projectiles, and long beams protruded from the rims. The wheels have been regular on pivots to allow for more facility of movement, and the tool have grow to be driven each with the resource of men in the machine and inside the returned of it, with a complete of 3,400 guys required to move it. Demetrius the Besieger, whose forces had been those laying siege to Rhodes, moreover constructed extra penthouses to defend his siege engineers, and the severa tremendous siege engines he already had at his disposal. In coaching for the attack, Demetrius also had the land inside the the front of the Rhodian walls cleared (Diodorus Siculus, XX, 91).

Chapter 7: Evan Mason's diagram of the Helepolis

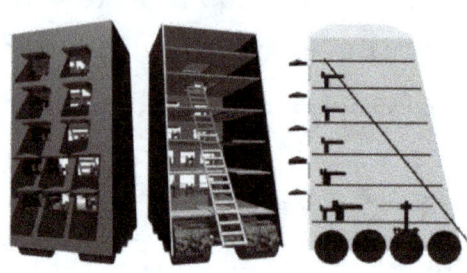

Demetrius changed into unsuccessful in his ambition to seize Rhodes, irrespective of the helepolis. After the siege, it turned into dismantled by means of manner of manner of the Rhodesians and its plate have end up melted right all of the manner down to make contributions to the improvement of the famous Colossus. The Assyrians had used siege towers earlier than the Greeks however the helepolis have end up the most crucial and maximum ambitious of its day, and the inspiration for the incredible siege towers of the Romans.

The Sambuca come to be an armored siege ladder which transferred squaddies to the enemy's wall. The ladder balanced on a pyramid-shaped mount with the useful resource of a pivot and changed into weighted with the useful resource of a place of lead at one forestall. The other surrender supported an assault platform with a door that modified into pulled up with ropes. The mount moved on wheels, and inner men grew to grow to be a large screw that moved the ladder to the specified function. The ladder itself become enclosed and guarded via way of wicker and materials much like folks who protected unique engines inclusive of the tortoise and helepolis.

The ancient Greeks furthermore superior hundreds of ballistic engines that would assail town partitions, collectively with an arrow-firing catapult used inside the Siege of Motyla in 397 BCE. This engine appears to have been modeled on the crossbow or gastraphetes, a much in advance invention of the Greeks from the 5th century. The gastraphetes or "belly-releaser" modified into established on a stock and cocked through resting it at the floor with a hollow area on the give up of the stock pressing into the stomach.

The oxybeles used at Motyla had been fast supplanted through larger and more effective catapults, in conjunction with the engine invented through Zopyrus of Tarentum inside the fifth century, that might fireside 2 heavy bolts and come to be cocked with the resource of manner of a windlass. The catapult of Isidoros of Abydos have become over 12 ft lengthy and could fireplace stone balls weighing as a lot as 40 kilos.

The palintonos of Diades became the notable howitzer of its day, recognition about 20 toes tall and hurling huge projectiles. The relevant beam become cocked by way of a powerful winch and held in region by using the use of the usage of ratchets. The big fingers that held the string had been supported by the usage of an cutting-edge pair of torsion springs. The monagon employed via the use of the Macedonian military moreover hurled large stones, but by using using a joist supported thru using a torsion spring. It modified into cocked via a rope wound round an axle grew to grow to be by means of the usage of manner of handspikes.

The historical Greeks did not invent Greek fireplace, the mysterious liquid fireplace used by the Byzantines that burned on water, but they did use incendiary guns. Pitch, oil, resin, sulfur, quicklime and animal fats were all used, no longer first-rate with the useful resource of the Greeks but via many historic armies. However, the

Greeks completed engineering technology to their use in siege struggle. In the Peloponnesian War (431-404 BCE), which the Spartans fought within the path of Athens and its allies, the Boeotian League employed an resourceful engine including a hollowed out beam, positive in iron, mounted on a 4-wheeled carriage. At the rear end of the beam have become a large bellows on the equal time as a metal bucket changed into suspended on the the the front. This bucket or cauldron contained a aggregate of burning coal, pitch, and sulfur, saved continuously aflame with the resource of the use of the bellows blowing air via a metallic that curved into it. When the bellows modified into labored difficult first-rate flames were created that burned wooden walls and their defenders. This horrible flamethrower changed into moreover changed to crack stone by way of manner of the addition of materials along side urine and vinegar.

The maximum first-rate weapon in Greek facts modified into probable an invention of Archimedes, for this massive of Greek arithmetic and engineering constructed a working cannon 1,500 years earlier than they were first hired in European conflict. It consisted of a metallic cylinder encased in a wood barrel, supported via a tripod: 2 spiked legs raising it midway down the barrel and some different pole sticking out from the rear. The pinnacle of the barrel have end up blocked through a wooden joist. The backside forestall of the barrel come to be an empty chamber heated with the resource of a hearth beneath. When the air within the chamber reached a certain temperature, the valve containing water opened and emptied itself into the chamber. The water may additionally need to right away evaporate and fire a stone ball resting inside the metallic cylinder.

Leonardo da Vinci recreated this weapon in the late fifteenth century, attributing it to Archimedes and known as it the Archinoterre. The cannonball apparently weighed almost 70 kilos, and present day-day reconstructions of the cannon have tested that it had various up to at the least one,250 ft. When the Industrial Revolution got here, numerous tries have been made to deliver a cannon fired thru steam, and all of them have been unsuccessful. In reality, it grow to be not till the Second World War that the Holman manufacturing business enterprise made a steam operated weapon in the United Kingdom, an anti-plane gun. Even then, it could only aim low-flying aircraft at about three hundred feet.

Another mysterious invention attributed to Archimedes is variously stated in historical property with such grandiose names as "The Ship-Shaker," "The Snatcher," and the "Iron Hand," however today it's far excellent known as Archimedes Claw. Whatever it looked like, it modified into a very precise weapon that became never eventually replicated by means of a few different civilization, at the side of the Romans. That has led many to doubt its very lifestyles, however the historic historians described it especially element. For example, Polybius wrote, "Other machines invented with the resource of Archimedes have been directed in competition to the assault activities as they superior under the shelter of video display units which blanketed them in competition to the missiles shot via the partitions. Against those attackers the machines ought to discharge stones heavy enough to pressure decrease returned the marines from the bows of the ships; at the equal time a grappling-iron linked to a chain is probably allow down, and with this the person controlling the beam might also need to take keep of on the supply. As fast as the prow became securely gripped, the lever of the device in the wall might be pressed down. When the operator had lifted up the supply's prow in this way and made her stand on her stern, he made rapid the lower factors of the tool, simply so they may not glide, and ultimately with the resource of a rope and pulley abruptly slackened the grappling-iron and the chain. The end result changed into that a number of the vessels heeled over and fell on the perimeters, and others capsized, at the identical time as the majority whilst their bows have been permit fall from a top plunged below water and filled, and consequently threw all into confusion. Marcellus' operations have been as a result clearly pissed off with the useful resource of those improvements of

Archimedes, and on the equal time as he saw that the garrison no longer best repulsed his attacks with heavy losses but also laughed at his efforts, he took his defeat difficult. At the equal time he could not refrain from developing a funny story in competition to himself whilst he stated: 'Archimedes uses my ships to ladle sea-water into his wine-cups, however my sambuca band were whipped out of the wine-party as intruders!' So ended the efforts to seize Syracuse from the sea."

Similarly, Plutarch described the effects of the Claw: "At the same time huge beams have been run out from the walls so that you can project over the Roman ships: a number of them had been then sunk by using awesome weights dropped from above, on the equal time as others had been seized at the bows via the usage of iron claws or through beaks like the ones of cranes, hauled into the air through counterweights until they stood upright upon their sterns, and then allowed to plunge to the bottom, in any other case they had been spun round via windlasses positioned in the metropolis and dashed in competition to the steep cliffs and rocks which jutted out below the walls, with amazing loss of lifestyles to the crews. Often there could be seen the terrifying spectacle of a deliver being lifted smooth out of the water into the air and whirled about as it hung there, till each man had been shaken out of the hull and thrown in first-rate course, after which it is probably

dashed down empty upon the partitions."

Giulio Parigi's painting of the Claw

Experimental archaeologists have constantly been inquisitive about the concept of the Archimedes Claw. They have been capable of recreate cutting-edge reproductions of the Claw that worked, primarily based upon clinical estimates of the generation that turned into to be had to Archimedes. According to the historic assets and demonstrations of achievable reproductions, the Claw changed into developed with the useful resource of Archimedes in some unspecified time in the future of the siege of Syracuse especially to counter the chance of a Roman naval attack. In essence, the Claw operated like a massive crane, each the usage of a giant counterweight or organizations of fellows and oxen to haul on a cable. This cable (probable an anchor cable from one of the

Syracusan quinquiremes, probably manufactured from Nile papyrus, an incredibly resilient cloth) turn out to be threaded via a crane arm and became tipped with the useful resource of way of a huge iron grapnel, customary like a claw.

It is uncertain whether or not or no longer the claw come to be hinged and for this reason designed to understand, just like a cutting-edge crane's grapnel, or whether or not or not it changed into genuinely a barbed lump of iron, but in every case, its motive grow to be smooth. The Snatcher modified into established at the ramparts overlooking the harbour with its arm extending over the waters of the slim bottleneck that gave get proper of access to to Syracuse's covered docks. Once an enemy deliver sailed internal range under it, the Claw will be dropped onto its decks, at which aspect really certainly one of severa effects might be anticipated. The

Claw may harm thru the smooth middle of the deliver, developing a hole beneath the waterline that might assist sink it as soon because the Claw changed into withdrawn. Otherwise, the Claw ought to tangle with the deliver's rigging, ultimately of which the defenders could start the usage of counterweights that could virtually supply the deliver out of the water severa feet in the air, probable shake it, and then drop it decrease back into the ocean. This massive marvel may want to either pull apart the person planks which made up the deliver's hull, letting in a flood of seawater, or tip the deliver onto its factor, causing it to swiftly sink.

However he designed it (assuming he did), the Claw proved to be a devastatingly effective weapon, a lot in order that no matter a huge numerical superiority, the Roman navy emerge as by no means able to breach the Syracusan harbour regardless of blockading it for over years. Polybius also defined a comparable machine Archimedes seemingly concocted to deal with Roman infantry too: "At the equal time Appius Claudius Pulcher found himself faced with similar difficulties whilst he attacked with the useful resource of land, and ultimately he abandoned the strive. While his troops were though at a distance from the walls they suffered many casualties from the mangonels and catapults. This artillery have end up relatively powerful each within the quantity of its fireplace, as turn out to be to be expected on the identical time as Hiero had furnished the materials, and Archimedes designed the severa engines. Then, even though the soldiers did get close to the wall, they were so compelled through the volleys of arrows and darts which always poured via the embrasures, as I described above, that their support have become correctly halted. Alternatively, within the event that they attacked under cowl in their penthouses, they have been crushed thru the stones and beams which have been dropped on their heads. The defenders moreover killed many men through the iron grappling-hooks allow down from cranes, which I said in advance: those were used to elevate up guys, armour and all, and then allow them to drop. In the stop Pulcher withdrew to his camp and summoned a council of the military tribunes, at which it emerge as unanimously determined to use a few different techniques in region of persist in the try to seize Syracuse with the aid of manner of typhoon. And this resolution was never reversed, for at some point of the 8 months' siege of the city which followed, despite the truth that they left no stratagem or formidable try untried, they in no way all over again ventured to mount a giant assault. So actual it's far that the genius of one man can emerge as a large, nearly a exquisite asset, if it's far nicely carried out to superb issues. In this case, at any price, the Romans, having delivered up such severa forces every with the aid of sea and via manner of manner of land, had every desire of taking photos the town right away, if simplest one antique man out of all the Syracusans could have been removed; but as long as he grow to be gift they did not dare even to try an assault with the aid of any approach which made it viable for Archimedes to oppose them."

Despite its progressive nature, the Claw changed into a reasonably number one mechanical tool, but a number of Archimedes' different designs were so great that to these days the debate maintains as to whether or not or no longer they ever existed the least bit. Archimedes' use of mirrors is probably the maximum contentious of his "improvements".

The use of mirrors is first said through Lucian, who wrote about the siege of Syracuse more than 3 centuries later, and it changed into eventually referred to as overdue as the mid-400s AD via Anthemius, a Greek student who published a take a look at entitled On Burning Glasses. Cassius Dio, every other Greek historian who lived all through the early 0.33 century A.D., additionally may moreover have stated it in passing. An edited model of Cassius Dio's data (edited with the aid of way of way of a medieval creator named Zonaras) stated, "Marcellus crossed into Sicily and proceeded to besiege Syracuse. The town had submitted to him, however then had revolted once more because the quit result of a fake message sent through the treachery of certain men. Now he could have subdued it very directly, because the result of a joint assault upon the wall through way of land and sea, had no longer Archimedes alongside along along with his improvements enabled the inhabitants to resist for a completely long time. For this guy with the aid of his devices suspended stones and heavy-armed infantrymen in the air, and those he would possibly permit down all at once, and presently draw them up all over again. And he might boost up ships, even the ones equipped with towers, by way of manner of other appliances which he dropped upon them; and raising them aloft, ought to permit them to drop all at once, so that once they fell into the water they were sunk with the resource of the use of the effect. At very last in an great manner he burned up the whole Roman fleet. For by way of tilting a form of replicate in the direction of the solar he targeted the sun's beam upon it; and due to the thickness and smoothness of the mirror he ignited the air from this beam and kindled a exceptional flame, the whole of which he directed upon the ships that lay at anchor inside the route of the fireside, until he consumed all of them."

A medieval Byzantine writer named Tzetzes wrote about the mirrors even more descriptively nearly 1500 years once they have been allegedly used: "Archimedes constructed a kind of hexagonal reflect, and at an c language proportionate to the dimensions of the reflect, he set comparable small mirrors with 4 edges, transferring with the useful resource of hyperlinks and through a kind of hinge, and made the glass the centre of the sun's beams ... So after that, even as the beams were pondered into this, a terrible kindling of flame arose upon the ships, and he reduced them to ashes a bow-shot off."

According to Lucian and Anthemius, during the siege of Syracuse, Archimedes devised a warm temperature-ray that would in fact set Roman ships on fireside from a large distance. Although many had been skeptical of these assertions in some unspecified time in the future of statistics, numerous contemporary experiments (which consist of maximum lately on Mythbusters) have met with a severa diploma of achievement in recreating a "warm temperature ray" utilising substances that could were available to Archimedes. The resources theorized that Archimedes' Mirror have become a chain of mirrors made from hammered silver or bronze polished to a immoderate sheen and positioned upon the battlements on a rotating base. If the rays of these mirrors, when they contemplated the sun, were aimed in a focused fashion at precisely the right attitude, the ones might also need to theoretically have generated sufficient warmness to achieve over 570° Fahrenheit, heat enough to ignite the timber Roman ships.

The idea of a "warm temperature ray" has captured the imagination of humans for plenty of years, and Rene Descartes himself taken into consideration the opportunity of the warmth ray earlier than finding it fantastic. One cutting-edge take a look at upon wooden which have been liberally treated with flammable pitch (as Roman ships could have been, because it have become utilized in caulking and absorbed with the aid of the wooden) resulted in the wood igniting. Other tests were tons less a hit and sincerely produced a minimum, localized amount of charring, although it is able to be argued that even a small amount of fireside and flames must short spiral out of manage on an historic warfare-galley, in which actually every object on board have become extraordinarily flammable. Moreover, to people ignorant of the technology behind the phenomenon, the sight of their ships' timbers igniting for no feasible reason have become prone to be a terrifying experience.

With that said, it appears no longer going that Archimedes devised a warm temperature ray. The greater modern-day ancient assets meticulously defined the siege guns and defenses, however they said not whatever about the use of mirrors.

Chapter 8: Buildings and Other Structures

One of the maximum famous factors of Roman engineering modified into their discovery and development of concrete and cement. The Roman call for concrete became opus caementicium, and this cloth come to be essentially based totally on hydraulic-placing cement. Its superb sturdiness is cited now to be in large part due to the addition of pozzolanic ash to the bottom combination, which averted any cracks from spreading. Concrete modified into being significantly utilized by the number one century CE, and its numerous kinds allowed the Romans to construct more structurally complicated homes than formerly imagined or tried.[3] One of the clearest examples of that is the development layout and formation of the arch.

The aggregate of fabric development and architectural improvement brought approximately severa knock-on improvements in transportation, conversation, military fulfillment and the capability to effectively Romanize conquered territories. Further advances in developing street networks and in managing water assets contributed significantly to securing Rome's function inside the historic international, and all of this enabled the Romans to not only depart a protracted lasting legacy every in phrases of bodily houses, systems and roads, but moreover designs and thoughts.

The Romans generally confronted any concrete form with bricks, and the concrete itself consisted of aggregates that were generally a ways large than in current concrete. This supposed that it have turn out to be typically laid in place of poured, as is the norm nowadays.[4] The aggregates utilized by the Romans, however, did range and will encompass portions of rock, ceramic tile, and brick rubble. Nevertheless, Roman concrete will be very a whole lot similar to what's used in recent times, being crafted from an aggregate, a hydraulic mortar, and a binder (commonly gypsum and quicklime) blended with water that hardens over time. Pozzolana changed into usually used anywhere feasible. With such excessive concentrations of alumina and silica in pozzolanic mortar, it's miles this progressive factor that made Roman concrete masses more proof towards salt water than maximum modern-day types. Pozzolanic cement is similar with contemporary Portland cement, moreover excessive in silica content material, and mirrors cutting-edge cement to which blast furnace slag, fly ash, or silica fume had been introduced. [5]

Most significantly, the Romans observed the way to put together concrete that might set below water, and this changed into key to the development of bridges and houses that were located alongside riverbanks and waterways. The metropolis of Caesarea offers the earliest examples of this underwater concrete generation getting used on a big scale. It is not appeared exactly when this shape of concrete became first observed, however by using the usage of spherical one hundred fifty BCE it become being used frequently in manufacturing in some unspecified time in the destiny of the Italian Peninsula, leading a few historians to remember its actual discovery may also date once more to the third century BCE.[6]

Writing round 25 BCE, Vitruvius (80-15 BCE) in his Ten Books on Architecture identified the only of a type aggregates that have to be used for lime mortars, recommending that pozzolana and pulvis puteolanus have to be carried out in a ratio of one:three lime to pozzolana for cement for constructing introduction and a 1:2 ratio for underwater work. It is a testomony to the Roman's technical prowess that those aggregates are very similar to the ratios although utilized in contemporary concrete.[7] The sturdiness and strength of Roman underwater concrete became based totally totally totally on the fact that seawater reacted with the ash and quicklime to create tobermorite, a substance that turn out to be found via using the Romans which minimized fractures. For some present day analysts, this produced "the most long lasting constructing cloth in human statistics."[8]

Emperor Nero (37-68 CE) changed into accountable for stimulating a massive a part of the brick and urban industries following the outbreak of the Great Fire in sixty four that destroyed a lot of the city of Rome. Alongside this, he end up additionally liable for introducing a strict building code that required all new systems to be constructed of concrete and faced with brick.[9] The entire of Italy is susceptible to earthquakes, so the concrete used had to have the ability to stand as much as excessive strain and be flexible enough to hold the integrity of the buildings. The mixture of concrete and bricks have become able to meet the ones conditions and lets in offer an motive for why such loads of historic Roman houses are nevertheless popularity.[10]

One new form that Romans started to use concrete for emerge as the introduction of large domes. Prior to the perfection of the dome, architects confronted the complex problem of supporting a heavy stone roof. It became idea that the high-quality answer became to construct severa columns and enhance the partitions. However, this did now not meet the other essential issue for Roman shape: to be an aesthetically stunning structure. Before Roman innovation in this region, even houses that had been terrific at the out of doors were darkish, constrained regions internally. Conversely, Roman domes created indoors vicinity that grow to be spacious and open.[11] The development came from Roman statistics of the arch and a cognizance that the ones same ideas may be circled into 3 dimensions to create a form that had the identical supportive strength over a terrific big area. Of route, with out concrete, this concept would possibly have remained precisely that.

Over time Roman engineers located that they may build big and stronger domes thru various the factors of the concrete used. For example, the Pantheon turned into constructed with the mixture of the better dome being made from light tuff and pumice, giving the concrete a density 80 4 lb./cu ft., whilst travertine as an combination emerge as used within the foundations, giving a density of 140 lb./cu ft.[12] Modern assessments of Roman concrete have led a few engineers to undergo in mind the use of Roman techniques within the education of concrete, changing the volcanic ash with coal fly ash. The advantages are that fly ash is 60% tons less luxurious and leaves a extensively smaller environmental footprint because of its lower cooking temperature and lots longer lifespan.[13] When coupling this with modern-day examples of Roman concrete which have been subjected to harsh marine environments and are showing little signs of wear and tear and tear and tear but having been decided courting decrease returned to over 2,000 years vintage, it appears a practical method to some of the issues faced nowadays in terms of weather alternate and environmental erosion.

The dome of the Pantheon, which spans an extraordinary 40 three.Four meters, have end up not matched for properly over a millennium. It represents a culmination of the Roman architectural revolution delivered to fruition in some unspecified time inside the destiny of the path of the first century CE in large element because of the adoption of amazing concrete,[14] which modified into properly-perfect to the improvement of curvilinear architectural bureaucracy. Indeed, the dome of Hadrian's Pantheon grow to be so technologically superior that it come to be now not capable of be considerably surpassed till the modern technology started out to use metal and reinforced concrete as building materials.

An indoors view of the rotunda dome

Chapter 9: Giovanni Paolo Panini's 18th century portray of the interior

Even to fashionable architects, the dome of the Pantheon stays some thing of an enigma. There isn't any evidence of brick arch facilitates within the dome (anticipate in its lowest aspect), so the best manner in which Roman builders built the Pantheon's dome has in no way been decided. Nevertheless, architects have recognized the two elements crucial to its achievement: the awesome excellent of the mortar used in its concrete and the cautious selection and grading of the mixture fabric.[15] Additionally, the uppermost 0.33 of the walls' drums (as seen from the out of doors), which coincides with the decrease part of the dome (as seen from the inner), allows to contain the thrust with internal brick arches. Brick arches and piers set above every different inside the 6 meter thick partitions help to strengthen the drum itself. The Pantheon's rotunda became equal in top and radius to the cylinder underneath.[16]

The frame of the Pantheon because of this consisted of a revolutionary incredible circular area. Its indoors end up constructed with a controlling geometry based definitely mostly on an incredible imperative axis. Its horizontally and vertically aligned coffers have been marked off by using way of coffers that have been aligned horizontally and vertically over the sloping floor of the dome, and people culminated in an oculus of superb dimension. This oculus have

become centrally located over the indoors area and poised over the vital circle inside the pavement.

Pictures of the oculus inside the middle of the dome

The place of the Pantheon's rotunda changed into illuminated simplest via the usage of the slight that pours via this eight

meter oculus beginning reduce into the center of the dome.[17] This singular supply of mild for the complete building become in the beginning topped with an intricate bronze cornice, which became in all likelihood also gilded. Nineteenth century art work historians who devoted their lives to the have a have a look at of the Pantheon boast of the manner they had set up its "100 ninety unwell-conditioned steps, and gazed down upon its substantial vicinity via the 'eye' of the summit. Standing almost inside the centre of the building, it's far a view which may be termed with literal accuracy 'lousy' as you perceive the surface on that you stand trending some distance from beneath you, an abyss spreading an extended way away on every element; you may almost fancy your self status on a cloud 'within the third heaven.'"

The discovery and improvement of concrete, then, is going hand in hand with the Roman improvement of the architectural layout of arches. They can't stake declare to the genuine invention, with the primary arch seeming to had been an innovation of the Etruscans,[18] however arches got here to be prominently used at a few level in the Roman Empire and have been architectural talents in themselves. Arches had been taken into consideration to be aesthetically fascinating to Romans and have been frequently used at the aspect of Greek architectural designs and talents which include columns, capitals, architraves, and pediments to create the top notch Classical fashion this is nonetheless so well-known.

That stated, the architectural importance of arches may be observed more in their service as the foundation of numerous outstanding Roman houses. Basically, arches reinforced and supported building systems. Their gain comes from their form; it's far their curve that allows systems to unfold weight from above, all the manner all the way right down to the ground, through pillars that manual the arch. As properly because the primary arch, vaults and barrel vaults, which can be essentially longer arches, enabled even big, heavier, tasks to be undertaken. For example, barrel vaults had been a selected feature placed in Roman bathhouses. They had been used right right here now not just because of their strength however moreover due to the fact, now not like traditional masonry the usage of timber for the roof, barrel arches had been evidence in the direction of decay and had been minimally laid low with the immoderate humidity, which made them ideally suited to such environments.

The big form of Roman houses that characteristic arches is legion, however the maximum well-known is the Colosseum, later named the Flavian Amphitheatre in honor of the own family who had it commissioned. It modified into started out through Vespasian in some unspecified time in the future of his reign (sixty nine-79) and finished with the aid of using way of his son Titus in 80. It had 80 arched entrances, and the entire edifice is probably nearly absolutely intact nowadays if now not for the vandalism and destruction over the years from robbers and those who used it as a available quarry.

Others arches famous for their elegance consist of the Arch of Septimius Severus, built in 203 at the Capitoline Hill and growing to 70 ft high, and the slighter smaller Arch of Titus, which grow to be constructed in 80 one with the useful resource of Domitian in honor of his brother and changed into 50 feet immoderate and built at the japanese element of the Forum. The Arch of Augustus became built in 29 BCE and became the number one of the various

Triumphal Arches constructed within the route of the Roman Empire. The closing predominant Triumphal Arch end up that of Constantine, built in 315, which stood at eighty 5 toes immoderate and is situated between the Colosseum and the Palatine Hill.

Carole Raddato's photo of the Arch of Titus

Impressive as those Triumphal Arches had been, arguably a superb extra critical use of the arch in terms of the broader populace is positioned in its affiliation with the aqueduct. Roman aqueducts have been absolutely vital within the boom of Rome itself, further to in the numerous cities the Romans primarily based completely at some point of the empire. The first diagnosed Roman aqueduct dates to 312 BCE, the Aqua Appia, and it modified into commissioned thru the use of the censors Plautius and Caecus. Rome come to be sooner or later furnished with the aid of way of as lots as 19 aqueducts, offering over one million cubic meters of water every day and which continues to be enough for over three million human beings in the modern-day-day city.[19] The blended duration of these aqueducts changed into over 2 hundred miles, and the Aqua Virgo, an aqueduct constructed with the aid of Agrippa in 19 BCE at some point of Augustus's reign, in spite of the truth that materials water to Rome's famous Trevi Fountain.

Chapter 10: A photograph of a part of the aqueduct

Along with the principle introduction, a number of sizable improvements may be seen with regards making sure the exquisite of the water furnished. Most aqueduct structures blanketed sedimentation tanks to lessen particles, along factor a machine of sluices (castella aquae). Stopcocks controlled the supply of water to character locations and overflows were stored in cisterns. Public fountains took priority over public baths, however each took priority over components to rich, fee-paying private customers. Showing themselves to be very lots aware about the need for recycling, the wastewater from aqueducts changed into used to water gardens or smooth the drains and public sewers. All Roman arches had been built using a series of arches and pillars that had a sluggish slope using gravity to ensure a consistent go together with the go with the float of water from mountain springs. After it had long gone through the aqueduct, the water became accrued in tanks and fed to its final vacation spot. This water furnished consuming water in houses, water for enterprise use, tub houses and sanitation, as well as the more decorative functions inside the various metropolis fountains. At its peak, Rome had a population of over 1.Five million people, and with out this massive water tool, it absolutely could not have functioned as a town.

While the Romans have been in reality amongst the primary to harness the strength of water and skip it freely at some point of the empire, they did not give you the real invention of the aqueduct. There are examples in India and Egypt that predate the ones of Rome. However, what the Romans did have grow to be understand the potential of the unique idea and then massively decorate upon it.[20] Even through cutting-edge requirements, the ones reconceived aqueducts had been exceptional feats of engineering but are even extra excellent while considered in the context of the historical international. They needed to be planned meticulously and regularly concerned a complex device of pipes, tunnels, canals, and bridges. New aqueduct systems have been constructed over a period of 500 years, from 312 BCE to 226 CE. Some had been financed with the aid of the united states on the instigation of a selected emperor along with Augustus, Caligula, and Trajan but non-public people or businesses of personal buyers moreover paid for structures, such modified into the recognition of their use and benefit.[21]

With the benefits of concrete and the improvement of the arch, Rome grow to be capable of construct incredible public homes to glorify their private metropolis and its population, as well to show their dominance and can inside the important cities inside the route of their conquered territories. Cities grew due to the fact water became available however a knock-on effect turn out to be that residents required increasingly more inside the way of infrastructure to satisfy their developing dreams. For instance, many circuses had been constructed inside the direction of the empire and provided venues for the gladiatorial contests, chariot races and amazing animal indicates that many Romans observed as their proper as imperial citizens.

The rounded stone arches of many aqueducts can still be visible at some stage in Europe, but those bridged structures made up only a totally small type of the masses of aqueducts that have been constructed in the path of the empire. The maximum critical aqueducts in Rome were the Aqua Claudia and the Aqua Marcia, which, together with the Aqua Anio Novus and the Aqua Anio Vetus, are seemed due to the fact the "four high-quality aqueducts of Rome."[22] The Claudia modified into started via Emperor Caligula in 38 CE and finished thru Emperor Claudius in fifty CE. The Aqua Marcia is one of the longest aqueducts. Built among 144-a hundred and forty BCE finally of the Roman Republic, this has the distinction of being the primary aqueduct to go into Rome on arches.[23]

What is frequently not favored is that maximum of the aqueducts have been in reality constructed under the floor, with best notably little in their period built on visible arches. With estimates suggesting that simplest five% of the water carried along the aqueducts really exceeded over bridges, many aqueducts had been truly massive engineering responsibilities, at the side of the aqueduct built thru the Romans to provide water to the metropolis of Carthage, which have come to be a hundred and ten miles extended.[24] Indeed, the Romans found progressive answers to all sorts of introduction troubles for their aqueducts. For example, in which depressions greater than 50 meters needed to be crossed, they used inverted siphons to push water uphill, and at Barbegal they constructed a complicated of water turbines described as "the high-quality stated hobby of mechanical electricity within the historical international."[25] Maintenance changed proper right into a constant problem, due to the fact the channels of aqueducts were liable to erosion from the water flowing via. To manipulate that scenario, the Romans developed eroding plaster, known as opus signinum, which used crushed terracotta within the everyday Roman mortar mixture of pozzolana rock and lime.[26]

Details for the constructing and manage of aqueducts comes in large aspect from the beneficial writings of Sextus Julius Frontinus (forty-103 CE). Frontinus loved a a achievement profession as a trendy underneath Domitian earlier than taking over the duty of the water commissioner in 90 seven, which noticed him end up at once answerable for the overseeing of Rome´s aqueducts. He wrote a very specific assessment of Rome´s tool that appears to have been written as a report to both Nerva or Trajan, entitled De aquaeductu. Included had been severa information approximately each the kingdom of the machine and guidance on safety. The volumes provide a entire statistics of the improvement of the machine, discharge costs, and the way the system functioned within the 1st century CE. The individual histories of all of the 9 aqueducts of Rome which have been in existence at the time of writing, consisting of sizes and discharge expenses, are indexed one by one: the Aqua Marcia, Aqua Appia, Aqua Alsietina, Aqua Tepula, Anio Vetus, Anio Novus, Aqua Virgo, Aqua Claudia and Aqua Augusta. Not simplest is there an define of the whole water-deliver tool of Rome, Frontinus additionally statistics the numerous prison pointers regarding its use and maintenance, as well as information concerning the tremendous of water being delivered through every of the aqueducts.

One of the primary motives for the document become for Frontinus to provide a sequence of targeted maps of the whole water tool from which destiny art work and a programme of protection might be deliberate and finished. From the ones he changed into capable of find one of the critical deliver problems: farmers stealing water through right now diverting it out of the gadget for their personal goals. Frontinus changed into capable of discover exactly in which such thefts were going on and took steps to cast off any unlawful pipes that have been attached. In addition, all jail pipes were now formally stamped and recorded.

Another problem highlighted via Frontinus's investigations changed into leakage, which end up specially difficult to deal with in underground sections. He and his engineers had been some of the number one to apprehend that trees positioned close to aqueducts should right away reason cracks, which then brought about leaks developing.

In line with Roman way of life, Frontinus used all of the facts that modified into to be had to him and relied carefully at the art work via way of Vitruvius.[27] Frontinus turn out to be succesful to plan the device within the sort of manner that water may be graded and allocated in line with whether it have turn out to be to be used for irrigation, gardens, and flushing (lowest notable), or reserved for eating water (maximum exceptional). Intermediate-tremendous water became despatched to baths and fountains. By keeping the numerous water assets simply separate, this enabled future engineers to make sure that the nice grade is probably checked and maintained.

The Romans protected complicated mathematical ideas into their major buildings, and this workout in itself demonstrates the technical sophistication in their engineers. For example, the idea of quality numbers is obvious inside the format of the Pantheon, with 28 coffers in the dome. The amount 28 is considered to be an extraordinary variety because of the truth its factors of 1, 2, 4, 7, and 14 brought collectively equal 28. Perfect numbers are uncommon, and their use is always planned and concept out.[28] Despite such fantastic architectural masterpieces constructed at some stage in the empire no matter the reality that, the names of maximum individual architects are unknown. This is maximum in all likelihood a give up end result of the Roman dependancy of inscribing the name of the person who had commissioned the building in place of the architect who designed it.

However, one architect who does come through strongly within the sources is Vitruvius. Originally a military engineer (praefectus fabrum), Vitruvius modified into hired with the aid of using Julius Caesar from 58-51 BCE and is thought to have designed some of homes in Rome.

Bringing together his non-public designs alongside layout mind from throughout the Mediterranean global, he gathered his architectural theories in his 10 extent paintings, De architectura, likely written among 30 and 15 BCE. It is the primary appeared most important art work on Roman shape.

Vitruvius started out with identifying what he considered to be Greek shape. His evaluation have become continuously primarily based mostly on mathematics, philosophy, arts, and social welfare, and he regarded structure due to the fact the unification of the arts and the sciences. For him, it modified into this aggregate that became the inspiration of the proper society. More importantly from a technological mind-set, he defined architectural concept and referred to that balance, usefulness, and beauty - what got here to be known as the "Vitruvian Triad" -

have been the cornerstones of shape. Through this paintings, Vitruvius basically created the theoretical method to shape, showed it as an academic and innovative career, and described the fundamentals of Western structure which might be nonetheless relevant nowadays.[29]

Many architects accompanied on the designs of Vitruvius within the ever-growing and ever-renovated town of Rome. However, handiest but another comes near Vitruvius in phrases of lasting recognition. Alive at some stage inside the second century CE, Apollodorus of Damascus become additionally a army engineer through schooling. In his ability as consul in ninety one, Trajan called Apollodorus to Rome, wherein he went without delay to emerge as the extremely-contemporary emperor's favored architect. He have become commissioned to construct severa commemorative homes to honor Trajan's conquests every in Rome and during the empire.[30] His maximum well-known monument is Trajan's Column, a ninety eight-foot tall monument that recounts the statistics of Trajan's victory over the Dacians. The awesome reliefs are an exquisite combination of beauty and generation used together to inform a tale. His unique fantastic project become Trajan's Forum, which became the final notable dialogue board to be built in Rome.[31]

A photograph of Trajan's column

After Trajan's lack of existence, his successor Hadrian showed himself to be each different avid enthusiast inside the format of systems. For Hadrian, structure become the epitome of schooling, thoughts, and sophistication.[32] However, now not all Roman architects were capable of bring together on such grand scales. The tremendous populace of Rome needed to be housed, and concept changed into given to greater normal homes too. The towns of Pompeii and Herculaneum provide precise statistics approximately the homes of greater middle-beauty Romans due to their burial thru the eruption of Vesuvius in seventy nine CE. The lava engulfing them has supposed they had been uniquely preserved and archaeologists are able to examine in fantastic element what dwelling situations had been definitely like for extra ordinary Romans.

The commonplace historic Roman residence of the middle commands appears to had been divided proper into a the the front area that was partly blanketed, known as an atrium, and a center area that became definitely blanketed, known as a tablinum. There became then an adjacent open court docket docket surrounded with the aid of columns called peristyles. These three additives had been located inside the identical order in almost every Roman residence of the Imperial period. Other smaller rooms have been then constructed round them in quite some techniques. The atrium have become a specially Roman function and is amazing to some thing seen in Greek shape. The rectangular area changed into protected with the aid of a roof projecting from the 4 partitions and had a rectangular starting left within the middle. In this remarkable form, the atrium emerge as known as the tuscanium and, which include to their invention of the arch, became probable Etruscan in foundation.[33] The pinnacle center splendor had variations of these homes, but residential regions were no longer strictly segregated in the same way as extra metropolis structures are nowadays. Large mansions owned with the resource of the usage of the richest (known as a domus) were built right besides the insulae that housed a number of the poorest inside the city.[34]

For the majority of the running-elegance population, domestic come to be residing in an insula, coming from the Latin term for island.[35] At the peak of Rome´s population, as an awful lot as 1,000,000 humans lived in such insulae, housing both plebs and some of the decrease middle instructions.[36] The floor floor of an insula become generally used for taverns and stores, with living homes located above. Insulae had been generally given a selected name, generally that of the proprietor, to distinguish them from each other, and names regarded from inscriptions encompass "Vitaliana, Eurcapriana, Cuminiana, and Arriana Polliana."[37] It come to be now common, but, for an insula to be owned through way of severa humans. Those living within the ones apartment blocks paid a specific diploma of lease decided thru way of wherein inside the building the rental changed into and its period. The houses at the lower floors tended to be the biggest, with the very smallest (and most volatile), therefore the most inexpensive, being positioned on the very best floors.

Most insulae did have the luxurious of some deliver of going for walks water and sanitation however have been regularly constructed the usage of the most inexpensive substances which includes wood or dirt brick. Only later after the Great Fire did Rome emerge as a predominantly concrete city. Prior to this, buildings have been susceptible to fireplace and frequently collapsed. Before Augustus brought a maximum pinnacle of about 70 toes, blocks of insulae ought to have as much as 9 memories. The peak restrict end up decreased with the useful resource of a similarly 10 toes in later years.

The extensively huge Insula Felicles (or Felicula) modified into positioned near the Flaminian Circus in Regio IX, which Tertullian condemned for trying to seeking to emulate the houses of the gods.[38] Lauded as "the richest man in Rome," Marcus Licinius Crassus (c. A hundred and fifteen-fifty three BCE) owned many insulae in the metropolis and whilst one collapsed, his scholar Cicero claimed that he became satisfied that the disaster had passed off for the cause that he might be capable of charge better rents for homes within the new constructing than within the collapsed one.[39]

It is concept that a normal insula ought to accommodate over 40 human beings in approximately three,six hundred rectangular feet. One insula could comprise seven residences, every masking 1,000 square ft. One surviving insula in Rome has been found at the foot of the Capitoline Hill. Named Insula dell'Ara Coeli, it's miles a 5-tale building and has been dated to sometime at some stage in the second century CE.[40] Another extant instance of a more high-priced insula is at Ostia, moreover courting to the 2d century CE. It is not identified how not unusual this kind come to be, but it had a living location known as a medianum from which all the remarkable rooms have been accessed. The reception rooms were wonderful sizes at both quit and were partitioned in addition into separate rooms.[41] Glazed domestic windows supplied mild and unnoticed a garden. On each side of the medianum there were small rooms (cubiculī). In the instance at Ostia, the better floors had kitchens, latrines and piped water. The constructing changed into adorned with ornate pilasters or columns with outdoors doorways to staircases foremost as a whole lot because the apartments. The decorations propose that those who lived there have been from the wealthier instructions.

Records show among forty two,000 and forty six,000 insulae had been registered within the town through using the third century CE, in evaluation to about 2,000 domus. These homes for the poorer usually had badly-lit cells commencing without delay to a shared dwelling area, which included the latrine alongside the cistern for consuming water.[42] However, the character of the insulae with such cramped, overcrowded residing intended that the Romans needed to undergo in mind primary subjects which include sanitation. Once all over again, on the same time as the Romans did no longer invent plumbing or bathrooms, they notably improved on earlier structures, mainly that of the Minoans, and have been the primary to introduce flushing toilets.

Tied to the issue of popular hygiene, the Roman public baths, or thermae, rose from Roman innovation and technological development and finished an essential social and cultural characteristic. The baths had 4 additives, starting with the apodyterium or converting room. Next became the tepidarium or warmth room, wherein warmth-up and stretching carrying sports activities can be undertaken or wherein slaves oiled the bathers. The concept become to bring about sweating preceding to moving into the caldarium or hot room, which became specially heat and humid and often reached forty stages Celsius. There have emerge as typically a steam bathtub and a labrum (cold-water fountain) in right here. Finally, the frigidarium or bloodless room enabled bathers to take a cooling bloodless bathtub.[43]

The containment of warmth inside the rooms within the Roman baths emerge as vital to the whole operation. To save you doors from being left open, door posts had been set up at an inclined thoughts-set in order that the doors should automatically swing near. Another approach of heat efficiency end up the usage of wooden benches over stone, as timber conducts away a good deal less warmth. The wealthier Romans additionally addressed the problem of heating for their homes in iciness via inventing a machine which circulated hot air during the house thru hollow regions in columns. The warm air rose up thru the areas created, heating the house.[44] Until the advent of contemporary structures, the Roman method modified into the maximum green and powerful way of heating a domestic.

Chapter 11: Transportation and Communications

Major Roman houses have been constructed to remaining and had been frequently on the grand scale as they felt befitted their imperial reputation. However, in practical terms, it become their development of their street and verbal exchange networks that were in reality greater crucial in increasing and controlling any such large empire.

Although the Romans also can have perfected street constructing in the historic worldwide thru using a totally unique shape of concrete/pavement, they will have observed out the idea and a number of the techniques from incredible people before them. The historical Egyptians had been a number of the primary human beings in the historic international to create a complicated tool of roads in their empire, and that they known as their street gadget the Waut Heru ("Roads (or Ways) of Horus") (Gardiner 1920, 103). Modern students recognise about the Roads of Horus thru ancient Egyptian inscriptions left on the Temple of Karnak in Luxor, in addition to an historical ebook known as the Papyrus Anastasi I (Gardiner 1920, 113).

The roads, which may moreover have included loads of miles, linked the Egyptian fort of Sile inside the northeast Delta to the metropolis of Rafa in Gaza (Gardiner 1920, ninety nine). During the New Kingdom (ca. 1539-1075 BCE), the Egyptians created a powerful empire which have end up able to both rule without delay over the diverse town-states in Palestine and/or created change routes to that place to benefit unusual commodities which consist of cedar. The Roads of Horus also can had been so properly travelled that they were even written about inside the Bible: "And it got here to pass, whilst Pharaoh had allow the human beings circulate, that God led them not thru the Way of the land of the Philistines" (Exodus 13:17).

The number one cause of the Roads of Horus turn out to be to facilitate trade and to provide easy routes for the Egyptian navy to march into Palestine (Gardiner 1920, 115), and as such, the roads have been well-fortified with forts, entire with crenellated partitions, stationed alongside the manner (Gardiner 1920, a hundred and fifteen). Triumphal pharaonic stelae may additionally moreover have lined the roads if you want to emphasize the power of the Egyptian king and his navy, and moreover to mark the bounds in their domain (Gardiner 1920, 107). The Roads of Horus had been constructed for in easy terms pragmatic features – satisfaction trips did no longer exist on the time – and that have end up a sentiment echoed loads of years later when the Romans first constructed the Via Appia.

New archaeological evidence has observed that the maximum critical towns of the big neo-Assyrian Empire of the 8th and seventh centuries BCE were additionally related to the beneficial useful resource of a first rate community of roads. Since the Assyrian Empire became plenty vaster than the Egyptian New Kingdom (and Egypt emerge as really part of the Assyrian Empire in brief within the middle of the seventh century), the Assyrian road gadget became possibly lots greater superior than its Egyptian predecessor. For instance, there have been severa manner-stations alongside predominant routes that provided additives for the Assyrian army (Kuhrt 1995, 2:535).

The vast community of roads the Assyrians constructed turned into then later accompanied and introduced to via manner of the Achaemenid Persian Empire in the direction of the 7th-4th centuries BCE, and the fifth century BCE Greek historian Herodotus wrote an outline of the tool, acknowledged these days because the Persian Royal Roads, in his Histories: "At durations all along the street are recognized stations, with wonderful accommodations, and the road itself is steady to excursion with the aid of, as it in no way leaves inhabited u . S .." (Herodotus V.Fifty two). The maximum travelled and well-known of the Persian Royal Roads ran from Sardis in Anatolia (modern-day Turkey) to Susa in Persia (Brian 2002, 357), and the capitals of the Achaemenid Empire – Pasargadae, Persepolis, Susa, Babylon, and Ecbatana – had been all related collectively via roads in a hard quadrilateral (Briant 2002, 358).

The Persian Royal Road tool modified into seemingly a good buy greater sophisticated than the Egyptian Roads of Horus, even though a good buy of it was though primitive in comparison to the later Roman avenue device. A large labor strain became needed to bring together the Persian Royal Road tool, which become provided each through conscripted exertions or paid employee's known as kurtash (Briant 2002, 361). Although exertions became no longer a trouble in constructing the Persian Royal Roads, era turned into, because of the fact even as the Royal Roads had been constructed massive sufficient to cope with chariots and wagons, they have been no longer paved, which intended that dust roads have become swampy roads at the same time as it rained (Briant 2002, 361).

Although the roads of the Egyptians, Assyrians, and Persians might not be as well-known because the later Roman roads, they truly supplied a template for the Via Appia and all other next Roman roads. The pre-Roman roads of the historical international moreover tested that an inexperienced dual carriageway machine changed into essential in maintaining the communications, trade, and military strains open that gave existence to an empire. The Romans expounded on this, and maximum of the Romans' roads are though used across the world to this contemporary. In terms of design and manufacturing, they had been now not equaled, not to mention handed, till the past due 19th century.

Most Roman cities had been fashioned like a rectangular. There have been 4 essential roads important to the middle of the city, usually to the Forum. The roads formed a bypass form, and each element on the brink of the skip have grow to be a gateway into the town. Connecting to the ones fundamental roads were smaller roads, alongside which the city citizens lived. The Romans' ability to construct durable, right now roads is nicely documented, specifically highlighting the strategic blessings of allowing messages, cash, and troops to be moved fast and effectively at some level within the exquisite territories. As such, these civil engineering competencies contributed substantially to the expansion and control of the empire.

For most roads, the Romans used a combination of gravel, dust, and bricks in desire to sincerely the rocks and gravel used by particular street builders. The (re)invention of these specifically Roman roads started out in about 3 hundred BCE with the primary stretch of the Via Appia being completed in 312 BCE. This grow to be a massive building program that persisted to be added too, ultimately ensuing in over 50,000 miles of toll road with the useful resource of 100 and fifty CE, including the Via Postumia, which joined the Adriatic to the Tyrrhenian Sea and included Cisalpine Gaul.[45]

In addition to providing an green manner for the motion of armies, officials and civilians, similarly to a speedy way of sending respectable communications, Roman roads were furthermore vital in the development and renovation trade. Through a machine of numerous kinds of Roman roads, beginning from small network roads to important big highways, cities, towns, and military bases have been all able to be related. The large roads were commonly stone-paved and metaled, cambered for drainage, and accompanied via bridleways, drainage ditches and pedestrian paths. Believing that the shortest course amongst two elements end up constantly a right away line, road stays display that the Romans did now not permit herbal boundaries to discourage them from constructing their highways as right now as feasible. However, this aspiration introduced with it the want to increase new strategies in bridge constructing and for helping roads during marshy ground on rafted or piled foundations.[46]

Roman bridges had been constructed with stone and/or concrete and carried out the arch significantly. Roman engineers have been the number one to bring together bridges the usage of this shape of concrete, however this fabric emerge as no longer simply used again in the production of bridges till the nineteenth century. The biggest Roman bridge emerge as Trajan's bridge over the Danube that modified into built by way of his architect, Apollodorus of Damascus. Over three hundred hundred Roman stone bridges built strong sufficient to address visitors had been identified, further to 34 Roman wooden bridges and 54 Roman aqueduct bridges, a massive a part of which remains fame and nonetheless capable of deliver modern-day vehicles.[47] Further estimates keep in mind 931 Roman bridges, in particular of stone, constructed in 26 particular global places.[48]

Roman arch bridges were each semi-round or segmental. The segmental arch had the advantage that flood water need to pass beneath more resultseasily, permitting it to be lighter, and as a give up end result inexpensive. A huge characteristic of one of the crucial bridges in Rome, the Pons Fabricius, changed into its flood openings inside the piers. Built in sixty BCE, this is one of the oldest essential bridges in spite of the fact that status. The Limyra Bridge become constructed with 26 segmental arches with a mean span-to-rise ratio of 5.3:1 and a form now not bettered till modern-day times.[49] Trajan's bridge over the Danube had open-spandrel segmental arches made from wood and remained the longest arch bridge for a millennium. The designs of Roman arch bridges were based totally definitely mostly on the idea that the overall circle changed into the best form, indicating all over again that the Romans at the identical time as pragmatic have been furthermore interested in aesthetics.

Pascal Reusch's picture of the Pons Fabricius

At the height of the Roman Empire, 29 most important military highways ran from its capital, at the same time as the 113 provinces were related via the use of 372 crucial roads. The avenue community had 250,000 miles of roadways, of which 50,000 have been stone-paved.[50] In Gaul, over 13,000 miles of toll road had been constructed and Britain boasted over 2,500 miles, and a whole lot of the ones roads form the inspiration of current-day-day roads. The Via Egnatia associated the Adriatic with the Aegean and the Bosporus, at the identical time due to the fact the Via Domitia ran from the Alps, within the route of the Rhone, all of the way thru the Pyrenees into Spain. Way stations providing refreshments have been moreover maintained by way of the usage of the empire at normal durations alongside the ones roads, with a separate machine of converting stations for professional and private couriers that enabled a dispatch to excursion a maximum of 500 miles in 24 hours through the usage of a relay of horses.

As seen with their arches and columns, it modified into all through the reigns of the Flavians, mainly Trajan and Hadrian, that Rome reached the height of strategic imperial road building. However, the number one emperors were moreover early avid avenue builders. Augustus, for instance, rebuilt the Via Flaminia in 27 BCE, and Claudius finished the mission began with the resource of his father Drusus to construct a street right thru the Alps. Governors and different provincial leaders took their cues from the ones emperors and additionally initiated number one avenue building packages, which includes Agrippa (sixty 3-12 BCE), who constructed a road from Lugdunum, contemporary Lyons, to the English Channel. Territories had been, in impact, boxed in with a crisscross of roadways on a large scale. The time period limites changed into on the begin a surveyor's time period for the course that marked the boundary between plots of land, but ultimately got here to mean the frontier works of the empire.[51]

The Itinerarium Antonini Augusti is a valuable historical deliver, almost unique in its data and detail.[52] It is largely a sign up of all of the stations and distances alongside numerous roads primarily based on a survey executed below Augustus:[53] "With the exception of a few outlying portions, which incorporates Britain north of the Wall, Dacia, and high pleasant provinces east of the Euphrates, the complete Empire end up penetrated by means of manner of manner of those itinera. There is hardly ever a district to which we would anticipate a Roman exquisite to be sent, on provider either civil or military, where we do now not find out roads. They attain the Wall in Britain; run along the Rhine, the Danube, and the Euphrates; and cover, as with a community, the interior provinces of the empire."[54]

The roads had been built through digging a pit along the direction all the way right all the way down to the bedrock, which became then filled with rocks, gravel, or sand. A layer of concrete protected the ditch and became finished via being paved with polygonal rock slabs or bricks. The bricks used were crafted from volcanic granite and gave strength to the roads. In addition to the invention of this sturdy combination, the Romans furthermore came up with the concept of banks on the edges to save you the rainwater from flooding the toll road. With their in-constructed proof against floods and special environmental dangers, they have been so well-designed and built that many have been however in use over 1000 years after the fall of the empire.

New techniques to construct bridges have been devised even as vital to finish a street. Similarly, tunnel building furthermore arose from a realistic want for roads and aqueducts to observe their meant course. Building a tunnel is in no manner smooth, and the whole procedure regularly took years, in big detail due to the truth surveyors had to make certain that every ends of a tunnel met efficiently inside the middle. For instance, the six-kilometer tunnel constructed with the resource of Claudius in forty one CE took 11 years and 30,000 humans to build.[55] The Romans progressed upon the "qanat" method, first superior via the Persians in the 1st century BCE. Tunnels had been made without delay with the useful resource of the use of a line of posts laid over a hill and thru digging vertical shafts at normal intervals. The shafts ensured that the tunnel line did not deviate, and further they furnished air go with the float to the human beings. This technique of production required meticulous making plans and a whole statistics of surveying and geometry, which Roman engineers had. Ventilation, particularly in very long tunnels, changed into a amazing trouble as shafts couldn't be excavated effortlessly in mountains. When the rock that changed into being dug out was hard, the Romans used an modern method of fireside-quenching or hearth-setting, which involved heating the rock after which cooling it fast with cold water to activate cracks.[56]

The huge networks of roadways were used to disseminate statistics similarly to preserve exchange and troops. The Romans completed a device of circulating written information and proper notices via carving in stones or on steel which have been positioned in a public location. These slabs of stone were known as Acta Diurna (day by day acts/events). This device started out in fifty nine BCE and is credited to Julius Caesar.[57] The data contained in them became not numerous to that which might be positioned in modern-day-day newspapers, though the list of executions have become actually more particular to the Romans. They were compiled daily and had been installation on a board referred to as an Album. After final there for an less expensive time, they had been taken down and saved with distinctive public documents.[58]

In parallel with the improvement of roads, the Romans added the primary top notch use of milestones and signposts. Augustus notably applied the opportunity to inaugurate an empire-huge postal and courier service, the Cursus Publicus, which delivered administrative instructions or solutions to questions, or perhaps introduced officials.[59] This postal carrier changed into though running in the sixth century CE within the Byzantine Empire. Dissemination of data become similarly greater thru using the advent of the Codex, the first positive papyrus books. Again credited to Julius Caesar, this approach came to be used appreciably among others in numerous fields, on the aspect of through later Christians to make codices of the Bible. Historians go through in thoughts it to be the first instance of a modern-day e-book.[60]

The maximum crucial form of transportation used on the roads come to be the horse-drawn cart. The Romans devised specific carts for freight and drinks, referred to as barrel carts, which had large cylindrical barrels laid horizontally with their tops going via in advance. The maximum not unusual form of cart, no matter the fact that, modified into the plaustrum or plostrum, essentially a platform made from forums with solid wheels (tympana) that have been numerous inches thick. The facets have been constructed up with forums or rails, as critical, and from time to time a big wicker basket changed into located on it. A -wheeled version existed alongside aspect the everyday four-wheel kind referred to as the plaustrum maius. The navy used each a popular wagon and a cursus clabularis, which modified into thru and massive used to move the military's bags.

When heavier building substances, which includes sand or soil, have been needed to be moved for road or bridge constructing, this introduced about the format of carts with immoderate walls. In addition, a delivery tool using rails have turn out to be moreover advanced. The rails have been honestly grooves embedded into present day stone roadways and the carts used in this device had massive block axles and wood wheels with metal casings. The carts had been technologically state-of-the-art and had brakes, a suspension, and bearings. The suspension structures used leather-based-based totally belts connected to bronze supports to suspend the carriage above the axles, for that reason permitting a smoother journey for the passenger. The use of bearings changed into each different idea advanced from an precise concept with the beneficial useful resource of others, in this situation the Celts.